Clinical Studies in Transpersonal Psychotherapy

SUNY Series in
the Philosophy of Psychology

Michael Washburn, Editor

Clinical Studies
in
Transpersonal Psychotherapy

Seymour Boorstein, M.D.

Foreword by Ken Wilber

State University of New York Press

Production by Ruth Fisher
Marketing by Theresa Abad Swierzowski

Published by
State University of New York Press, Albany

© 1997 State University of New York

For information, address the State University of New York Press,
State University Plaza, Albany, NY 12246

Library of Congress Cataloging-in-Publication Data
Boorstein, Seymour.
    Clinical studies in transpersonal psychotherapy / Seymour
Boorstein, with a foreword by Ken Wilber.
        p.   cm. — (SUNY series in the philosophy of psychology)
    Includes bibliographical references and index.
    ISBN 0-7914-3333-1 (hc : alk. paper). — ISBN 0-7914-3334-X (pb :
alk. paper)
    1. Transpersonal psychotherapy.   I. Title.   II. Series.
    [DNLM: 1. Psychotherapy—methods.   2. Mental Disorders—therapy.
3. Psychoanalytic Theory.   WM 420 B724c 1997]
RC489.T75B66 1997
616.89'14—dc20
DNLM/DLC
for Library of Congress   96-23228
                                                                    CIP

10 9 8 7 6 5 4 3 2 1

This book is lovingly dedicated to my children and grandchildren:

Grace, Nathan, Erik, Leah, Collin, Emmy, Johan,

Peter, Trish, Liz, Hans, Michael, and

Sarah

Contents

Foreword by Ken Wilber   ix

Preface   xv

Acknowledgment   xvii

Introduction: Redefining Transpersonal Psychotherapy   1

Chapter 1:   *A Theoretical Framework for Transpersonal Psychotherapy*   15

Chapter 2:   *Introducing Transpersonal Interventions*   27

Chapter 3:   *The Transpersonal Treatment of Psychotic Disorders*   51

Chapter 4:   *The Transpersonal Treatment of the Borderline Psychotic Patient*   61

Chapter 5:   *The Transpersonal Treatment of Mood Disorders*   81

Chapter 6:   *The Transpersonal Treatment of Pre-Neurotic Character Disorders*   89

Chapter 7:   *The Transpersonal Treatment of Neurotic Illness*   105

Chapter 8:   *The Transpersonal Treatment of Existential Problems*   125

Chapter 9:   *Relationship Psychotherapy and*
             Spiritual Traditions   143

Chapter 10: *Conclusions*   173

Bibliography   179
Index   185

Foreword

by Ken Wilber

THERE SEEM TO BE THREE GENERAL PHASES—each lasting about a decade—that new schools of psychology go through in the course of their own growth and development: the first phase is one of innovation and extreme enthusiasm; the second, one of hard work and conceptual labor; the third, one of general acceptance and assimilation by mainstream schools (assuming it achieves any sort of acceptance at all). The first phase tends to be more enjoyable; the second phase, more productive; and the third, more rewarding.

I believe Transpersonal Psychology is now beginning its second major phase. It is moving from the enjoyable phase to the productive phase—the phase that, because it is marked by more intellectual rigor and integrity, is all the more vital and productive and, therefore, in its own way, all the more exciting.

The first phase began about twenty-five years ago, with the pioneering work of Huxley, Maslow, Watts, Sutich, and the founding of the *Journal of Transpersonal Psychology*. The atmosphere was one of electric excitement; the enthusiasm, almost palpable. There were grand visions in the air. Meditation, yoga, psychedelics, biofeedback—all had combined to literally blow open the field of psychology and introduce it to heights of consciousness—and depths of consciousness—never before dreamt of by Western science. The enthusiasm and excitement of this first phase was evidence of, and testament to, the genuine power that the new field of Transpersonal Psychology had tapped into and unleashed. No Western scientists had ever explored such vast new fields of mind and consciousness. We were all pioneers; we were both the subjects and the objects of our own investigations; above all, we were enthusiastic. The New Age lay before us.

I believe that giddy, happy time is over. If Transpersonal Psychology is to enter its second and more productive phase, that raw energy and enthusiasm must now be channeled, via coherent and systematic ideas, into a comprehensive and unified framework.

Above all, I believe this comprehensive framework must reach out to, and embrace, the orthodox and mainstream schools of psychology, and it must do so in a very rigorous and detailed fashion. It seems to me that only in this way can Transpersonal Psychology become the truly comprehensive school that it rightfully claims to be. Freudian psychoanalysis became the dominant school of psychiatry for half a century, not because it displaced earlier schools, but because it so effectively encompassed them that it rendered them almost superfluous. Freudian psychoanalysis, in other words, took as its foundation the then existing schools of psychology and psychiatry, and, by effectively incorporating their essential insights into its own system, became the dominant school of psychiatry for the next half-century.

I believe the same "grand synthesis" can and must now be accomplished by Transpersonal Psychology. And that means we must take very seriously the idea that orthodox psychiatry and psychology have already laid a viable foundation, but it is up to us to incorporate this foundation and then build on it to develop it into a much more comprehensive and transpersonal orientation.

One of the main tasks before us, then, in our productive phase, is the building of bridges between Transpersonal Psychology and the more orthodox, mainstream schools. There are, in my opinion, four major orthodox schools with which Transpersonal Psychology must contend: 1) Behaviorism—including not only classical and operant behaviorism, but also the more modern schools of cognitive behaviorism, social learning theory, and self-regulating management; 2) Neuro-physiological psychology—including neuropharmacology, brain research, and physiological psychology; 3) Psychoanalytic Psychiatry—including psychoanalytic ego psychology, object-relations theory, and self psychology; and 4) Cognitive Developmentalism—including the work of Piaget, Kohlberg, Gilligan, Loevinger, and Arieti.

In approaching these four major orthodox schools, we can take one of two views: we can assume the orthodox schools, because they lack a transpersonal perspective, are essentially wrong in most respects and therefore need to be replaced *in toto* by Transpersonal Psychology; or we can assume the orthodox schools are more or less correct as far as they go, but need to be supplemented with Transpersonal Psychology.

For various reasons, I think the second view is the only possible way to proceed. That is, I believe the major orthodox schools are essentially correct as far as they go, but they need desperately a supplement of the soul. They are correct but partial, and thus the job of Transpersonal Psychology is to build upon that orthodox foundation a more comprehensive, viable, and adequate psychology, one that includes not only mind and body but soul and spirit.

I believe this approach is the correct one with respect to all four orthodox schools—the behavioristic, the physiological, the psychoanalytic, and the developmental. With Behaviorism we can easily accept the central role of reinforcement theories and self-regulating strategies, but we must add the notion of higher levels or dimensions of reinforcement. An event becomes a reinforcer not only if it satisfies physical and emotional needs, but also if it satisfies mental, psychic, and spiritual needs, which are every bit as real as—indeed, more real than—the need for material food or sex. Our job is to incorporate behaviorism, not deny it.

Likewise, we can easily accommodate the central tenet of Physiological Psychology, namely, that every state of consciousness has a physiological correlate and that psychopathology may be (in whole or part) a physiological dysfunction partially correctable by pharmacological agents. Large sectors of modern psychiatry have, in fact, abandoned the strictly psychoanalytic model and embraced the physiological model—the so-called "medical model"—because its clinical results are so immediate and palpable—certain classes of anxiety, depression, phobias, and thought disorders yield almost immediately to pharmacological management. This medical or physiological model has been further bolstered by major break-throughs in the understanding of neuro-transmitter pathways and functions (such as acetylcholine, norepinephrine, the endorphins, and so forth). Underlying this entire enterprise is the assumption that each specific state of consciousness—and therefore, each specific psychopathology—has a specific physiological correlate, and, therefore, can be manipulated at a pharmacological level. All of this rests on the mapping and correlating of states of consciousness with their particular physiological substates.

Transpersonal Psychology would simply add that there is a whole spectrum of higher or transcendental states of consciousness; that the physiological correlates of those states can and should be mapped; and that those states might also be triggered, at least temporarily, by pharmacological action. Moreover, Transpersonal Psychology can do this without embracing the psycho-neural identity theory (which is a blatant form of reductionism); to say that higher states of consciousness leave their footprints in the physiological substratum is not to say these higher states are their footprints.

The third major orthodox school that Transpersonal Psychology should eventually embrace is the Psychoanalytic school. Unfortunately, psychoanalytic theory seems so profoundly antithetical to spiritual concerns that most transpersonal psychologists avoid it entirely. But, again, I believe the more accurate view is that psychoanalysis is not entirely incorrect nor inaccurate; rather, it contains some very important but very partial truths, and our task as transpersonal theorists is to incorporate these partial truths into a much more encompassing and adequate discipline.

Likewise with the fourth major orthodox school, that of Cognitive Developmentalism. Here, our job has been easy: we have agreed with the developmentalists that consciousness develops through a series of stages or structures. We have simply added that there are demonstrably higher stages of conscious development than those recognized by the orthodox. And this has been easy, as I said, because developmental-logic itself announces the necessity of higher, transcendental, or transpersonal states. Developmental-logic rests happy nowhere short of Infinity.

Here, then, is the task of Transpersonal Psychology in its second major phase, its productive phase: if Transpersonal Psychology is genuinely a psychology of Totality or Wholeness, then it must be able to foster a broad integration or general synthesis of the four major orthodox schools, by showing each school to be a correct but partial aspect of a larger truth; and it must then use this integration as the foundation upon which a more properly transcendental, spiritual, or transpersonal model can profitably be built.

I do not think this synthesis of orthodox schools is as formidable as might at first appear. Donald Hebb has already provided us with a key integrating link between the behavioristic and physiological models, namely, the idea of synaptic facilitation. A behavioristic-reinforcing event is a synaptic facilitating event. And Piaget has already provided us with a key integrating link between behaviorism and cognitive development, namely, the idea that an event can be reinforcing only if it can be assimilated by the organism and that levels of development are, therefore, actually levels of allowable reinforcers.

What remains, for the "grand synthesis," is an incorporation of modern psychoanalytic theory. I think the broad outlines of how to integrate psychoanalysis with the other major orthodox schools is reasonably straightforward: as consciousness develops through its various stages of allowable reinforcers, a developmental miscarriage (a maladaptive self-regulation, reinforcement, or synaptic facilitation) will result in a particular type or class of psychopathology. In other words, different levels of developmental miscarriage (or maladaptive reinforcement or synaptic facilitation) would result in qualitatively different types of psychopathology (which, in turn, would yield broadly to different types of pharmacological intervention). Different stages of cognitive development mean different levels of allowable reinforcers and mean different levels of psychopathology (each accompanied by a distinctive physiological footprint or synaptic array).

Now, modern psychoanalytic theory recognizes three general levels of psychopathology: psychotic, borderline, and neurotic. I have suggested adding the broad classes of existential pathologies and transpersonal pathologies. In other words, the entire spectrum of consciousness can also be viewed as a spectrum of possible patholo-gies, with each level possessing a distinct and different type of possi-ble pathology requiring distinct and different treatment modalities.

What is now so urgently needed is exactly this type of inter-facing between psychoanalytic developmental models and a broader transpersonal approach. In my opinion, this is the last major inter-face needed before Transpersonal Psychology can effect its compre-hensive foundation. There are, to my mind, three researchers in particular who are doing pioneering work in this area: Jack Engler, Dan Brown, and Seymour Boorstein. Examples of the work of Engler and Brown can be found in *Transformations of Consciousness*. This book is Boorstein's approach.

One of the central ideas of this book is that as consciousness develops from pre-personal to personal to transpersonal modes, dif-ferent types of pathologies can arise, each requiring a different type of treatment modality. Of the five major classes of psychopatholo-gy—namely, psychotic, borderline, neurotic, existential, and transpersonal—Seymour discusses the impact of meditation on four of them: psychotic, borderline, neurotic, and existential. This book makes three important points: 1) in general, the treatment modali-ties for these pathologies are quite different; 2) in general, intensive meditation is contraindicated for the more severe and primitive pathologies (psychotic and borderline); and 3) there are, however, certain cases of primitive pathologies that appear to be helped by meditation (or other transpersonal exercises). Exactly what that means and how that occurs (if, in fact, it does occur) will remain a central point of theoretical debate for years to come.

Transpersonal Psychology has completed its first phase; we are now moving into the second or productive phase. In many ways, I think this phase is more exciting and even more visionary than the first. I believe extraordinary theoretical and clinical breakthroughs now lie in our collective grasp. If we meet the challenges ahead with intellectual integrity and rigor, I believe Transpersonal Psychology will take its rightful place as the sanest, the most basic, and the most comprehensive psychology yet to appear. If there is only one Self—and there is—there is only one psychology. That Self is transpersonal; and so, therefore, is that psychology.

Preface

THIS BOOK HAS HAD THREE SHIFTS IN EMPHASIS since I began it in 1984. Although at that time I had been practicing psychotherapy for twenty-five years, it was only in the five years prior to 1984 that I had begun to recommend transpersonal practices (meditation, philosophic study) to my patients. Recommending these practices as an adjunct to psychotherapy was the result of my own personal experience. My meditation practice had elucidated and resolved certain psychological conflicts that had not been resolved by the long personal psychoanalysis that was part of my training. I found philosophical studies valuable because they addressed the existential issues of purpose and meaning which were becoming increasingly important to me. My initial experiences of recommending these practices to patients were generally very positive, often dramatically enhancing the therapeutic results. Initially, I did not analyze precisely why these practices were effective or exactly how they worked to potentiate therapeutic progress. I believe that I may have thought that the technique itself had some inherent curative effect.

As time passed, it became clearer to me that spiritual techniques were differentially useful to patients relative to their levels of psychological health. I began to be able to discriminate which of the many component parts of complex, sophisticated spiritual practices (feeling group inclusion, identification with venerable teachers, alignment with a virtuous lifestyle as an ego ideal, transcending the illusory boundary between oneself and all creation) were the relevant curative factors for a particular person. Spiritual practice, I continued to believe, was beneficial in most situations, but helpful in a much different way for a psychotic individual than for a highly functioning, mildly neurotic person (like myself). Most helpful to me during this period of redefining my work were the Self Psychology formulations of Heinz Kohut and his followers, which I elaborate on in the body of this book.

In more recent years, I have added to my understanding the enormous effect that my own positive feelings toward my patients have on the therapeutic process. Because I am convinced that my access to compassionate feelings has directly grown as my own spiritual understanding has deepened, this book would be neither honest nor complete without recognizing this as an important factor. Indeed, although I started to write this book to explain techniques offered *to* patients and carried out *by* patients, this awareness of the crucial importance of *my own* spiritual practice answers the question about what one can offer to patients uninterested in or disinclined toward spirituality. To whatever degree my personal practice keeps *me* loving, keeps *me* compassionate and empathic, to that degree therapy proceeds most effectively.

Dr. Lawrence Le Shan once told me a story about a communication between Freud and one of his students, Flugel, in 1938.

Flugel: Tell me Maestro, how does psychoanalysis really cure the patient?

Freud: At one moment during the analysis, the analyst loves the patient, the patient is able to know it, and the patient is cured.

I offer this book to my readers with gratitude and respect to my teachers of psychotherapy, to my spiritual teachers, and to all of my patients who, in sharing their lives with me, really taught me how to be a therapist.

Acknowledgment

I want to thank Martha Ley both for her valuable
editorial assistance and for her enthusiasm
for the project.

Introduction

Redefining Transpersonal
Psychotherapy

I THINK OF MYSELF as a transpersonal or spiritual therapist. My psychiatric training forty years ago was traditional, Freudian, psychoanalytically oriented psychotherapy, and I feel that my work with patients over the years using the insights from this tradition has been very successful. In addition, over the last twenty years, my own personal spiritual and philosophical search has led me to widen the context within which I perceive human growth and development.

This personal search has impelled me to explore a number of spiritual paths and to examine and practice a variety of meditation approaches. My appreciation of the variety and complexity of the states of consciousness available to us has increased, as well as my appreciation of the potential wisdom that can result from exploring them. As my interest in the exploration of these avenues of personal growth has increased, so also has my readiness to share this interest with my patients.

My view of transpersonal psychotherapy is that it builds upon and embraces the techniques and goals of traditional psychotherapy by broadening the conceptual framework within which we understand human growth. It should be noted that when we think of transpersonal theorists who are clinicians, the two giants who immediately come to mind are Carl Jung and Stanislav Grof. They have done and are doing much work to pave the transpersonal road we are traveling in psychotherapy. Jung brought to us terms

1

such as the "collective unconscious," which points to the sense of one-ness and which is, of course, missing in the Freudian theoretical background. Stan Grof has been a pioneer, with views of the transpersonal that are groundbreaking.

In my experience, from viewing my own life as well as those of my patients, as areas of intrapsychic conflict are resolved through psychotherapy, existential questions about the meaning and purpose of life become more prominent. I am very impressed with Ernest Becker's speculation in *The Denial of Death* that what we under-stand to be separate psychological symptoms have at their very foun-dation the fear of confronting our mortality as human beings. I am likewise impressed with Irvin Yalom's work, *Existential Psychotherapy*, in which he too suggests that a variety of mundane, apparently superficial, symptoms are masking the more fundamen-tal concerns that we all share about the meaning of existence, our questions about purpose, and our inability to face our own deaths.

Transpersonal psychology and psychotherapy address the broadest conceptualization possible of human psychological growth. This includes, along with comfort and gratification in one's relation-ship with self, family, work, and society, a recognition of the yearn-ing for meaning, purpose, and transcendence of self-consciousness that are a part of our nature. Transpersonal psychology and psy-chotherapy presuppose the existence of a spiritual dimension in human beings, and being a transpersonal therapist presupposes sharing this conviction. The field is not limited to any particular spiritual or religious system—it recognizes the validity of spiritual systems in general and the yearning for spiritual unfolding as one of the givens of human growth and development.

I don't believe that it is possible for a therapist, from a sim-ply clinical or analytical point of view, to decide to be a transperson-al therapist. I went from being a traditional therapist to being a transpersonal or spiritual therapist over a period of several years, during which time my own world view, my values, and my goals for myself all changed. It would not have been possible for me to become a transpersonal therapist simply because I heard that some-one else was doing it and it sounded like an effective thing to do. It required a change in my personal belief system. Likewise, it would not have been possible for me to continue as a traditional therapist once my values and goals for myself in life had changed.

In my life experience, my interest in transpersonal matters and in broadening traditional psychotherapy did not begin until I was forty years old. At that time, I was enjoying a successful professional career and a gratifying family life. Although I considered myself Jewish, I did not have a spiritual practice. Coinciding with my father's death (and probably with the beginning of my own middle age), I began to think more and more about what might be called existential concerns—the purpose and meaning of life.

Just at this time, in the early 1960s, there seemed to be in the entire American culture a renaissance of interest in metaphysical philosophy and spiritual practice. A wide variety of lectures and workshops became available, promising to give participants expanded awareness, psychic powers, and out-of-the-body experiences. For a number of years I attended as many of these workshops as I could, hoping primarily (it seems to me in retrospect) to tap into some source of psychic power or powers. I also read widely in the field of metaphysics.

After a number of years my interest shifted. Whereas my initial focus had been on the special gifts and powers that seemed available through meditation, as time went by I became more and more interested in how the experiences of altered states of consciousness could illuminate the functioning of the mind.

This shift in emphasis brought with it a shift in the studying I did. I lost interest in reading about spectacular psychic feats; instead, I began to read more of the spiritual literature of the world's great religions and to think of meditation more as a technique for development of the heart and mind than as a road to personal power. Most recently, I have been influenced strongly by the teachings of Ramana Maharshi (particularly as presented by his student, Arthur Osborne) and by the contemporary British philosopher, Douglas Harding.

In my personal, continued search for spiritual meaning, I reconnected with Judaism, a connection that has continued to deepen over the last decade. One of my significant teachers is Rabbi Zalman Schachter-Sholomi, a Rabbi in the Hasidic tradition. It was through him that I began to appreciate the mystical branch of Judaism—Hasidism—and also to realize the great teaching power in the stories told about famous Rebbes.

At about the same time that I became interested in studying religious traditions, I began meditating. Although Judaism does include meditation practices, these are not widely taught; so I practiced, for varying periods of time, several different meditational forms—the best known of these was Transcendental Meditation, a mantra meditation. Mantra meditations exist in all of the spiritual traditions that I know. They consist of the repeated recitation (silently or aloud) of a simple word or phrase. As the mind is brought to focus one-pointedly, predictable and measurable increases in an individual's level of relaxation and sense of well-being develop.

Some years after I began to practice mantra meditation, I was introduced to Vipassana (mindfulness) meditation, a form of Buddhist meditation practice that was brought to the United States from Southeast Asia and made popular by several American teachers. This form of meditation, often called insight or awareness meditation, is the practice of carefully noting the moment-to-moment changing processes of the mind and body. It is not a practice of one-pointed concentration, although some level of concentration is required to strengthen awareness development. One way of understanding the goal of this practice is to recognize that the technique reflects the insight that life is moment-to-moment experience in constant change. It is understood that suffering in life is largely a reflection of attempts to cling to pleasant experiences while warding off unpleasant experiences. The ability to perceive directly that life experience continuously changes, in spite of our attempts to have it otherwise, enables a person to live more fully in the moment.

In my experience, there are also short-term goals and benefits of meditation practice which, as I realized them for myself, moved me to suggest to many of my patients that they begin this practice as well under the guidance of a spiritual teacher. The initial focus in Vipassana meditation is on developing a minimal level of concentration by focusing, as continuously as possible, on the simple and neutral experience of breathing. Concentration practices, as

I have pointed out, are generally calming and relaxing. Even beginning practitioners of Vipassana meditation, without necessarily arriving at any profound spiritual insights, may experience immediate relief of tension.

Another aspect of Vipassana practice that is helpful to me and has prompted me in turn to recommend it to many of my patients is that learning and practicing the techniques often takes place in the context of an intensive meditation retreat. The rarefied atmosphere of a retreat setting, the sense of being removed and remote from one's familiar relationships and work patterns, the minimizing of external stimuli (reading, writing, and talking are discouraged), and the long periods of meditation practice that are encouraged all mitigate in favor of beginning to see quite clearly the habitual patterns in which one's mind works. Long before one arrives at "transpersonal" or spiritual insights, one has ample opportunity to view the ways in which particular worries and preoccupations continue to arise and how particular defense patterns come into play to ward off unpleasant thoughts or feelings.

I think one of the things that first attracted me to this practice was its close similarity to depth psychology. In successive periods of intensive meditation, I was able to observe my habitual thought patterns and the feelings that accompanied them. I could see that these patterns often reflected some of the unresolved issues of my childhood. Reexperiencing these thoughts and feelings within this context of understanding then led me to a more complete resolution of these conflicts. When some of my patients, at my suggestion, began to do this practice in retreat settings as well, I was able to see that the practice was helpful to them in the same way. It goes without saying that meditators are also encouraged to practice the meditation in their own homes, as part of their daily life when they return from their retreat.

I recommend Vipassana practice judiciously because this is an intense practice which, especially in retreat settings, might have the effect of breaking down ego defenses. By ego defenses I am referring to those particular maneuvers of the psyche that operate to keep material that would be unacceptable or frightening repressed from the conscious mind. From a strictly theoretical point of view, it seems that it would be most valuable to people with relatively integrated ego structures, who are relatively psychologically mature, and who could withstand both the stress of external stimulus deprivation and the internal emergence of formerly repressed thoughts and feelings. However, as will become clear from reading the case material that makes up the bulk of this book, I have recommended this practice to several people whose level of psychological development was somewhat more primitive. The practice also seemed helpful to those people, although I think its benefits were of a different variety than depth insights. As I present the case vignettes, I will elaborate my theories regarding how and why transpersonal or spiritual psychotherapy works (when it does) for patients whose symptoms reflect the various diagnostic categories.

Another particular practice within the Vipassana tradition is metta (lovingkindness) meditation. The metta meditation is basically a form of concentration meditation, and the formal practice is the repetition to oneself, silently, of a set of four sentences called "metta resolves." The sentences themselves express the hope that all beings, including oneself, be happy and free from suffering. One technique for preparing oneself for this practice is to acknowledge that it is likely that, either consciously or unconsciously, one is responsible for having caused pain to others. One acknowledges as well the pain involved in holding grudges against other people who have, consciously or unconsciously, caused pain to oneself. The cultivation of this kind of spaciousness of mind attenuates a harsh or overbearing superego. I believe that the ability to be more lenient with and to forgive the unskillful behavior of others is a prerequisite to being more tolerant of ourselves.

The metta practice proved to be very helpful to me, and I have suggested to some of my patients that they work with it, either as a part of Vipassana practice or as a separate technique. I generally recommend it to people who struggle with excessive feelings of anger. I often find that people who are critical of or angry at other people are very self-critical as well. As the stated goal of most patients in therapy is to feel better, I point out to them that it makes sense to try to let go of their anger. It is usually not difficult to help people realize that, although "righteous indignation" or anger is often an exciting energy, it is ultimately debilitating and self-defeating.

Many of my patients work in therapy with the realization that their parents were not as emotionally available to them as would have been desirable, and they struggle with feelings of anger and loss over this early life deprivation. Often, their later life relationships are maladaptive, since they expect to receive from adult partners in relationships the nurturance they did not receive from their parents in childhood. In order to move on to more adult behavior, they need to be able to let go of the hope and/or expectation that *all* their decades-old infantile needs will ever be met. To do this, they must come to terms with the anger they feel toward their parents, whether it's "appropriate" anger or not. Many of my patients have found *metta* meditation particularly helpful in resolving their angry feelings.

There is another aspect of *metta* practice that has been valuable to me in working with my patients. Each morning as I look at the schedule of people I am to see that day, I spend some minutes cultivating metta feelings toward each of them. I do this by visualizing each patient individually and repeating to myself the scriptural metta wishes: "May you be free from danger; may you have mental happiness; may you have physical happiness; may you have ease of well-being."

I believe that repeating this *metta* "prayer" realigns me with my helpful intent in working with people and that that realignment reinspires my work. It also reminds me of those people toward whom I might have some negative feelings. My awareness of this sometimes arises when I realize that my metta resolutions are less than wholehearted—this impels me to confront my ambivalences, to perhaps see some countertransference and/or transference issues I had been unaware of, which often then helps me be more emotionally available to all of my patients.

Several years after I was introduced to Vipassana practice, I discovered *A Course in Miracles*. The *Course* is a recently transcribed manual written in the Christian mystical tradition. It purports to be a restatement of the essence of Christian teaching, stressing the element of genuine forgiveness as the way of breaking down the barriers that separate people from each other and allowing the fundamental unity of the human spirit to become more apparent. The manual presents a theoretical overview, a metaphysical understanding, of all we experience as the created universe. In addition to whatever theoretical formulations the *Course* presents, the major emphasis of its practice is the presentation of an orderly sequence of exercises designed to promote forgiveness, leading to a more accurate perception of ultimate reality and an understanding of unity consciousness.

I have found that *A Course in Miracles* often appeals to patients whose backgrounds have included Christian religious practice, even (and perhaps especially) those for whom traditional practice has become unacceptable or unsatisfying. In *A Course in Miracles* "sin" is interpreted as ignorance or misinterpretation of our essential oneness with each other and with God consciousness, rather than as moral misbehavior. The *Course* also honors each individual soul's potential for experiencing unity or God consciousness, and I have especially noted its usefulness with patients who struggle with self-hatred or poor self-esteem.

Not everyone to whom I recommend *A Course in Miracles* finds it helpful. People with other than a Christian background, or people whose Christian background was demoralizing, sometimes are put off by the *Course*'s emphasis on Christian terminology. However, for those people for whom the terminology is comfortable, working with the *Course* has proven to be nurturing and gratifying, and this has enhanced their progress in psychotherapy.

In summary, what I am presenting in this book is my clinical experience with the addition of various techniques from spiritual traditions and the philosophy of spiritual understanding as enhancements to traditional psychotherapy. An overall view I hold is that the complete spectrum of human emotional development includes both the realm of interpersonal relationship and the realm of transpersonal understanding. Traditional psychotherapy strives to bring the individual to the highest level of psychological development possible. Spiritual understanding can be seen as the natural completion of personal psychological growth and development, as the way in which an individual comes to relate most fully to all of life experience.

In brief, I hold that traditional psychotherapy builds ego where there has been inadequate ego development and repairs ego where there has been neglect or abuse. In working with classical neurotic concerns, it resolves conflicts in the ego that inhibit normal and gratifying expression of instinctual drives. Transpersonal psychotherapy, in theory, should address post-neurotic issues, existential issues of purpose and meaning.

Another way of looking at this would be to see that there are two parallel roads to spiritual development. The task of the first road is to build ego and the other is to build "no-ego." This view may be helpful in conceptualizing how certain spiritual leaders with genuine spiritual accomplishments and experiences can do things that seem abusive and hurtful. If ego development, or development of the self, has not progressed sufficiently, then that person will have difficulty in integrating spiritual insights into his or her everyday life. Unresolved problems from earlier psychosexual stages (using the Freudian model) might then distort the actions that stemmed from what are inherently loving and caring spiritual insights. This is especially true with problems of unresolved narcissistic issues.

What I have discovered and aim to demonstrate in this book is that the addition of a spiritual context, and sometimes techniques derived from spiritual traditions, often has a salubrious effect on the course of therapy *at all levels of psychosexual development.*

One dimension of my case presentations will be the use of particular techniques that derive from spiritual traditions. In some instances, patients were interested enough to investigate the entire spiritual tradition or had already been practitioners of a particular religious tradition. In other instances, the techniques have been extracted from the tradition as a whole and introduced only as particular techniques to meet a specific need. In certain cases, I encouraged patients to try various meditative techniques. In other cases, I suggested that patients work with *A Course in Miracles.* Often I recommended that they read certain books, a practice I have come to call "bibliotherapy," as a way of introducing them to spiritual contexts and sparking their interest in specific techniques.

I also select teaching stories, which exist in all spiritual traditions that I know. The parables of Jesus are a Christian example of teaching stories; Hasidic stories and Sufi stories offer wisdom in witty and engaging ways. Being familiar with teaching stories from a variety of religious traditions, I tailor my choice of story to what would be most meaningful to a particular person. Telling a story that is part of a wisdom tradition, and presenting it in terms of its wisdom tradition, enables me to make an important point without setting myself up as the source of wisdom.

I feel that it will become clear to the reader that the second dimension of transpersonal psychotherapy, the context within which I understand what I am doing and within which my relationships to my patients is held, is probably the more important aspect. I believe the techniques themselves, while helpful, depend on my relationship with my patients and the way in which I understand the work we are doing together. This has been the most remarkable part of my own journey in transpersonal psychotherapy: as I have become more relaxed, more compassionate, and less anxious, I have been able to view my patients' dilemmas more as an aspect of their spiritual journey than a reflection of pathology. I find that I am engaged more fully and resourcefully in our shared enterprise—rather than suffering from "therapist burnout," I am increasingly delighted with my work and find myself energized at the end of a day.

How to Approach This Book as a Whole

There are many basic books that attempt to teach the *rudiments* of psychotherapy in most of the great psychotherapeutic traditions. Even in the different branches of psychoanalysis, there are many and differing texts attempting to teach the rudiments of psychotherapy. This is clearly a field where most of the learning is done in the clinical (patient-therapist) arena, where supervision and case conferences take place.

The field of transpersonal psychotherapy is still in its childhood with many, many differing approaches (see *Transpersonal Psychotherapy*, SUNY 1996). It would, therefore, be far beyond the scope of this book to present a *total* comprehensive system for psychotherapists. Rather, I have attempted to present my approach to integrating my knowledge of psychoanalytic, psychodynamic methods with a number of spiritual tools with which I am personally familiar. And wherever possible, I have tried to explain my theoretical understanding of my decisions.

My hope is that the psychotherapist readers, utilizing their own traditional approach, will either experiment with some of the spiritual tools I have used and/or experiment with others that they have read about or have personally found to be of value.

We all need enough modesty to view our work as "half-baked ideas" which are still in the evolutionary process. So let us be open to examine everything and throw out what does not make sense to us.

I recognize that genetic, physiologic, and biochemical factors are also important and have, therefore, integrated them in the case studies where appropriate.

Because this is not primarily a spiritual text, there is relatively little discussion of the paths to ego transcendence, which, in most spiritual traditions, is a necessary step on the way toward enlightenment (union with God or the many other appellations this is given). Here again, all of the great traditions have many texts to serve as guides and require direct "field work" under the supervision of a leader.

Ken Wilber (*A Brief History of Everything*) and Michael Washburn (*Transpersonal Psychology From a Psychoanalytic Perspective*) have laid out the general pathways from birth to enlightenment, and most of the great traditions also have some sort of step-by-step progression indicated in their approaches.

This Book is Directed at Four Categories of Therapist:

1. Beginning therapists who have a "traditional" orientation toward understanding and healing of patient problems and who might be open to the "spiritual dimension." By this I mean that they might have some curiosity or interest in how "spirituality" might be of help personally in their therapeutic endeavors and how it might help their clients or patients. Of course, to even be open to this possibility implies that some

aspect of the personality of the therapist already entertains interest in this area.

It is my hope that therapists in this group can see the outline of a traditional psychotherapeutic approach (the one that I most often refer to is the psychodynamic psychoanalytic approach—in particular, Self Psychology), its inarguable importance, and how techniques "borrowed" from the various traditions can help support this endeavor. I must emphasize the importance of a traditional psychotherapeutic grounding, probably before, or at least coincidental with, the addition of the spiritual dimension.

2. Beginning therapists with a spiritual tradition. Many psychotherapists are being trained in graduate schools that face a difficult-to-solve dilemma. In a relatively short time, these schools are called upon to teach students how to be effective therapists upon graduation and to acquaint them with the vast potpourri of spiritual traditions and techniques that exist. It is a difficult enough task to try to teach the art and science of psychotherapy in three to five years. Unfortunately, what all too often happens in the name of eclecticism is that many differing psychotherapy approaches are taught and, because of the time limitations, none is taught with enough depth.

Although my own training as a psychoanalyst is clearly *my* psychotherapy path, I am in no way saying that this is the path to choose. Rather, my plea is for the student to learn *thoroughly* at least one system of psychotherapy. That way, when facing a disturbed patient or client, the new therapist will have enough psychotherapeutic *armamentarium* to be sufficiently fortified for the task in front of him or her.

Transpersonal schools have an almost impossible task, having to introduce some sort of spiritual dimension into the fundamental psychotherapy work. In this book, I try to demonstrate the way in which *I* attempt to synthesize the traditional and spiritual dimensions.

I strongly believe that a traditional psychotherapy approach, hopefully with an added spiritual dimension, is crucial for resolving problems stemming from traumas and maladaptions that arise during the first five to ten years of our lives. I believe that doors can be opened with more than one key: if a psychological key will not yet turn the lock, a spiritual key may be the one to first open the door.

3. Seasoned traditional therapists who have had little or no interest or experience with the spiritual dimension. The spiritual dimension cannot be taught or entered into purely from an *intellectual* point of view. There must be some type of emotional longing or stirring—albeit initially perhaps only mild emotional curiosity. It is my impression that many experienced therapists may be wary of the spiritual dimension because it is such a big unknown and because it is illogical from a traditionalist's point of view. They may also experience some anxiety that, having mastered an entire body of psychotherapeutic knowledge over many years, they will need to discard it and replace it with something else.

To any of these therapists who have read this far, I want to assure you that all the effective psychotherapy tools you have amassed will continue to be needed and are, in fact, crucial if you are to add the spiritual dimension. I have discussed this with many psychotherapist colleagues with differing orientations from mine (e.g., Jungian, Gestalt) who feel exactly as I do in these matters.

To reiterate, I am convinced that it is crucial that a comprehensive system of dealing with emotionally disturbed people be mastered before (or at least coincidentally with) the addition of spiritual approaches or techniques.

I thus attempt in this book to present a comprehensive psychotherapeutic approach along with my underlying thinking in the theoretical area. How, when, and why I have added a spiritual dimension is also explained in the clinical studies.

4. For the experienced transpersonal psychotherapist. I would invite your reading this book to see if any of the approaches here add to your psychotherapy tools. Because this field is still in its childhood, in my opinion, I invite the therapist to

throw out, modify, or add to any of my ideas. We definitely need to be open to each others' concepts, to consider them, see what there is of value, and then reinforce, build on, or replace them with fresh insights.

I am hopeful that this book, with its presentations of the particular techniques that I have used, will be a gateway through which other therapists can enter and feel empowered to begin to introduce transpersonal ideas and transpersonal issues in working with their patients.

Chapter 1

A Theoretical Framework for Transpersonal Psychotherapy

I FEEL THAT MANY OF THE HEALING or therapeutic aspects of a spiritual or transpersonal approach can be understood by investigating human development through the ideas of Self Psychology. Self Psychology, an elaboration of and shifting emphasis from earlier Freudian psychoanalytic theory, was developed by Heinz Kohut. It has been increasingly appreciated in the last two decades, during which it has become well known. It is an interesting coincidence that during these same two decades transpersonal psychotherapy has also gained prominence.

In 1969, I completed my psychoanalytic training at a classically oriented training center. At that time, Freud's energic drive theory was the commonly accepted core of psychoanalytic practice. From this perspective, it is sexual and/or aggressive impulses struggling against superego-dampening counterforces that give rise to conflicts and neuroses. However, in my professional practice I often could not get my observations of how my patients became ill and recovered to fit the classical models I had been taught. For some time I found myself searching for other models that could help me better understand what I was observing. In the 1970s, when I "discovered" for myself the transpersonal or spiritual realm, and began to share this dimension with my patients, I did not have a theoretical comprehension of it.

My interest in Self Psychology began at a conference of the American Psychoanalytic Association. I attended a lecture on Self Psychology where the lecturer's opening words were: "In my prior incarnation I was a Freudian psychoanalyst. . . ." That comment impelled me to investigate Self Psychology. What I was to discover led me to the conclusion that the Self Psychology approach provides a scientific framework for understanding the effectiveness of transpersonal psychotherapy.

Self Psychologists postulate, with much supporting theoretical and clinical evidence, that in order for a person to become a happy and psychologically healthy individual he or she must have, starting very early in life, appropriately empathic, loving nurturers (usually parents) with two principal functions. The first of these functions is that of looking at and mirroring back to the baby its sense of pride and expansiveness. This, they posit, later leads to a healthy sense of ambition and assertiveness. The second function is to be available as idealized figures, having the function of giving the child a sense of connection with greatness, strength, and calm. The Self Psychologists further feel that we continue to need, throughout life, empathic responses from our families as well as from our peer groups to maintain psychological health. Self Psychologists feel that these "twinship" or "alter ego" relationships provide a sense of connectedness with others and that this in turn provides the energy from which skills, talents, and competency are developed.

I believe many individuals are attracted to the various spiritual traditions to try to heal themselves from early psychological traumas—and many are successful in doing just that. In the field of psychiatry these might be called "transference cures" (a term coined in the 1930s by Dr. Franz Alexander, a Freudian psychoanalyst). Although many psychoanalysts believe that at best this is a second-rate healing, the Self Psychologists do not. Many aspects of the great spiritual traditions have the same psychological elements available that the Self Psychologists say are necessary for mental health to flourish. Self Psychologists would understand an individual's belief in a Godhead or spiritual being as having a selfobject function (Rowe and MacIsaac, 31). For example, Christianity and Buddhism mirror individual love, empathy, and acceptance in Christ

Consciousness or radiant Buddha nature. In addition, spiritual leaders, as spokespersons for the various religious traditions, may provide enhanced self-identification. Idealization of relationships most often occurs with the actual originator of the tradition, such as the Buddha or Jesus, but may also be established with the contemporary representative of the tradition (e.g., guru, rabbi, priest, etc.). Here one can build psychological strength by identifying with the presumed strengths and virtues of people whose lives manifest the ideals of their traditions.

I want to emphasize that by looking for clinical understanding of how spiritual traditions operate and citing how elements of spiritual practice may address psychological difficulties, I in *no* way intend to diminish the importance of spiritually transformative experiences in their own right. Ken Wilber postulates in *Transformations of Consciousness* nine developmental stages from birth to sainthood or enlightenment. The early stages, "pre-spiritual," closely match the classical Western psychological stages delineated by Erik Erikson in "The Eight Stages of Man," in *Childhood and Society*. The later stages reflect the spiritual stages of transcendence of personal ego, realization of ultimate truths, and a sense of the purpose and meaning of life. It is therefore my belief that involvement in a spiritual tradition can positively affect *both* the "pre-spiritual" and spiritual stages at the same time. For example, practicing a spiritual tradition might diminish (through resolve) selfish behavior stemming from early psychological traumas and a damaged sense of self. Simultaneously (through meditation), it might clear the blockages to the realization of one's God consciousness.

Psychotherapy helps with the healing of the conventional personality. There seem to be distinct phases of personality development that are related in a continuum. Just as spiritual practice is often viewed as a path, psychotherapy can be thought of as a path toward a more mature and integrated personality. In this context, psychological development may be understood as a necessary precursor of genuine spiritual development. Both paths are clearly interrelated: as psychotherapy increases one's capacity for witnessing the contents of one's mind, so meditation increases ego strength by increasing one's capacity to be aware of changing mind states without being overwhelmed by emotional responses. Also, spiritual practices can lead to an intensification of concentration and calm, which facilitates traditional psychotherapy. One can also view the spiritual ascent as requiring certain amounts of emotional energy. Unresolved early conflicts and traumas can keep this emotional energy from being available for the spiritual ascent. Therefore, traditional psychotherapy may even be the crucial step to help a patient with his or her spiritual aspirations.

Three prominent Self Psychologists who are further developing the work of Kohut are Robert Stolorow, George Atwood, and Bernard Brandchaft. In their text, *Psychoanalytic Treatment—An Intersubjective Approach,* they describe what they characterize as a "field" that exists between the patient and the therapist. Growth and change are perceived as products of that field dynamic. These authors emphasize the importance of the therapist's awareness of his or her thoughts and feelings about the patient and about the use of feedback from this awareness to maintain sincere empathy with the patient. It is provocative to consider how this emphasis on empathic response as a key factor in therapy is similar to practices of developing compassion that are part of many religious traditions. In the Self Psychology system, healing comes about through the experience of feeling valued and truly understood—the empathic bond is one of non-alienation, inclusion, non-separateness. Spiritual traditions might call this awareness the recognition of the "kinship of all beings" or the "interrelatedness of all beings."

If we accept the Stolorow, Atwood, and Brandchaft view that an intersubjective field is created by the interplay of the subjective worlds of the patient and therapist, the deliberate cultivation of compassion by the therapist can surely affect the course of therapy. One might even theorize, using this framework, that the therapist's practice of developing compassion makes treatment more effective even if religious ideas or spiritual practices are never specifically introduced.

Surely there are many compassionate therapists who do not think of themselves as religious and do not practice specific transpersonal techniques. However, for those therapists who are drawn to them, spiritual traditions offer specific meditation practices that promote the development of compassion. One example of this is the *Chenrezi* Meditation from the Tibetan Buddhist tradition. In this practice, the meditator envisions the particular Tibetan deity that symbolizes compassion and resolves to develop this quality within him- or herself (Khyentse, 85ff).

The common positive developmental factor for small children, psychiatric patients, and spiritual aspirants is a mature type of caring or love. There is the entire spectrum of love: from the way a small baby "loves" its mother to fulfill its needs to the universal selfless love of the saint or (truly) holy person. Between these two extremes, there are the many stages through which most ordinary people progress. As therapists, it is important to ask ourselves, "Is my action coming from my heart (from genuine compassion) or from some more infantile need?" Perhaps we do not ask ourselves, our therapists, or our spiritual leaders this question often enough.

As a partial antidote to these types of problems, the spiritual traditions specifically emphasize the development of crucial moral values. Examples from Buddhism include the "Right Speech," "Right Action," and "Right Livelihood" aspects of the Eightfold Path for enlightenment. Likewise, the Ten Commandments form a cornerstone of Judeo-Christian practice. Furthermore, both Buddhism and Christianity emphasize the development of compassion and forgiveness.

My spiritual practice has increased my attentiveness to my inner feelings. Retrospectively, I am aware that in my medical and psychiatric career I might not always have been as caring and thoughtful as I should have been toward my patients. I may have given myself the excuse that I was too tired or that the patient was too needy or bothersome. My spiritual practice has obliged me (and helped me) to see things differently. All true spiritual paths I know of emphasize the development of compassion, based on the spiritual insight of the interrelatedness of all sentient beings. An image I personally find helpful is that of a rhizome, a tuberous root that burrows underground and perennially sends up stalks. From above the ground, the stalks look separate. Underground, they are interconnected, and all are part of the same plant. In that vein, a line from *A Course in Miracles* that is particularly meaningful to me is,

"I and my brothers are one with God." For a period of time I practiced this line as a personal mantra. When I find myself sitting across from a patient in an interaction that is particularly difficult, that line often occurs to me spontaneously. Having it come to mind reminds me that a larger perspective on the interaction at hand is available to me, one in which my patient and I are lovingly involved in mutual work, as opposed to being two distinct individuals attacking a thorny problem.

Another image, from the Jungian tradition, is that of an underground stream that forms the wellspring of rivers. Ira Progoff, a Jungian psychologist developed the technique of personal journal keeping as a psychological tool. In his book *At a Journal Workshop,* he put forth the view that each individual's life is an idiosyncratic experience just as each person's well in their own backyard is his or her personal well. Individual wells in the same neighborhood would differ according to whose backyards they were in. Fundamentally, however, they would all draw water from the same underground stream.

In Buddhism, the insight of the awareness of suffering in all existence is used as a meditation to foster compassion. Several fundamental aspects of Buddhist practice may be used to expand compassion. The first of these might be the reflection on the fact that pain in life is inescapable. One develops the awareness that the very fact of having a physical body, subject to recurrent normal needs and periodic aches, creates pain. One may also focus on the awareness that in relational lives the experiences of grief and loss are inescapable. These two awarenesses often arouse a sense of sympathy for the other and for oneself. People are often relieved to find that life is difficult by its very nature, and not because of anything they are doing wrong. Also, when people understand how much the inevitable pains of life are magnified by struggling to change things that cannot be changed, their relationship to their lives and problems becomes less stressful, and they thus sometimes become less demanding of others. On occasion I may encourage patients to use the reflection, "Just as I wish to be free of suffering, so do all beings wish to be free of suffering."

If a spiritual path can lead to this broader perception, it may make it easier to transcend our own petty selfishness. We may become aware that when we help others we are, at some level, directly helping ourselves. I have found that compassion, like love, increases as you "give it away" and directly leads to feelings of well-being, greater self-respect, happiness, and, therefore, greater energy. The feelings of "being taken from," often categorized as "therapist burnout," are lessened and are then replaced by an appreciation of the privilege of helping others. At the end of a long work day, one can feel emotionally fulfilled even though physically tired. Whereas in the past I might have given up on certain "problem" patients, I now continue to struggle on, often with positive results. Both in my personal and professional life, I have found that this approach usually leads to positive feedback such as love and respect—things we all need to keep our emotional equilibrium.

It is appropriate to mention here that, along with the many potential benefits from the addition of the transpersonal dimension to psychotherapy, there are possible pitfalls. There are acknowledged hazards in spiritual practice which, unheeded, might emerge in transpersonal psychotherapy. In situations where an individual's basic personality is not well integrated, the practice of certain spiritual techniques may lead to unhealthy consequences. For example, certain meditational practices may help a person develop extraordinary psychic abilities. These "powers" have sometimes been erroneously equated with the development of genuine spirituality. While it is true that special talents do sometimes emerge as a byproduct of meditation practice, it is also true that these "powers" may naturally be present in individuals whose levels of personal and spiritual development are not remarkable.

This was probably the case with D.D. Home, a mid-nineteenth-century English psychic who was said to have acquired large sums of money from bereaved widows for helping them "communicate" with their deceased husbands. Jim Jones, the charismatic minister who led his Jonestown congregation to mass suicide, was believed (in this case, erroneously) to have clairvoyant abilities, and this belief gave him power over his followers. The blind devotion that Jim Jones seemed to inspire reflected, I believe, the search for a figure to idealize (and/or obtain grandiose mirroring from) to compensate for the lack of such a figure in one's own childhood. In fact, over-idealizing one's spiritual teacher is probably quite common. When this over-idealization is met by infantile counter-needs on the part of the teacher, difficulties may arise. On the other hand, under the aegis of a mature and integrated ego, these abilities or powers, when present, may be useful in helping others.

It is not unusual to find that therapists are also often idealized by their patients, much as a guru would be, with similar problems arising. Unfortunately, there have been many occasions both in spiritual traditions and in the field of psychotherapy when the needs of the spiritual aspirant or patient have become secondary to the immature needs of the spiritual leader or therapist. The adulation and idealization that come from the spiritual aspirant feed the leader's (or therapist's) remnants of his or her pathologic narcissism. This is quite similar to instances of parents who use their children to meet the unmet needs of their own childhoods. These are real dangers which must be recognized—the small child, the psychiatric patient, and the spiritual aspirant are all similarly vulnerable. They can be helped to grow via a loving, empathic approach, or they can be severely damaged by an unloving, hostile approach. The degree to which the parent, psychotherapist, or spiritual leader is genuinely, non-selfishly interested in the development of the child, patient, or spiritual aspirant will be directly reflected in the effectiveness of the outcome.

The Ethics of the Introduction of Transpersonal Issues with Classical Therapy

There has been considerable discussion in traditional psychology circles about the ethicality of introducing transpersonal issues into classical therapy. A major issue, vigorously debated when I was a psychiatric resident forty years ago, was whether revealing one's own value system to one's patients was inappropriately manipulative. It is understood in medicine that people generally respect their doctors and therefore may be more vulnerable to proselytizing on the part of their physicians. I do believe that all physicians, including psychiatrists, may have a certain persuasiveness in terms of the suggestions they make to their patients, based on the esteem in which they are held. Assuming that physicians, including psychiatrists, are motivated by sincere concern for their patients' well-being, I am not apprehensive about this "edge of persuasiveness." For instance, I feel comfortable about physicians sharing with their patients their concerns about cigarette smoking, based on their conviction that it leads to poor health. I feel no concern about whether this inhibits the patient's ability to "make up his or her own mind."

Similarly, I have no misgivings about psychotherapists raising with their patients important issues such as meaning in life, purpose, and the desire to understand why things are the way they are. In fact, I feel that not to raise these issues is to avoid looking at probably the central factor in psychological functioning. Because I share this view about the fundamental significance of these existential issues, I do not feel at all inhibited about opening up the possibility of pursuing spiritual paths to my patients. It goes without saying that I use a certain amount of caution in doing so. When I take the initial history of a patient, I am careful to inquire about his or her religious background, including spiritual beliefs and practices. I explore whether these issues seem of current importance. With individuals who do not consider that they are relevant in their lives, where their struggles and difficulties seem to be closely related to mundane issues, I use a fairly traditional, psychodynamically oriented psychotherapy approach.

Another reason I feel no ethical conflict about raising transpersonal or spiritual issues with my patients is that I clearly see a difference between introducing these issues as areas meriting consideration and an attempt, covert or overt, to persuade a patient that there is only one correct or superior spiritual path. When spiritual issues do seem relevant, I usually encourage the people I work with to explore them within the context of the spiritual path that has been part of their lives. Where positive feelings exist regarding the spiritual practice of one's childhood (or of one's adulthood when such spiritual practice has endured), it makes sense that this same practice will be most comforting and most rewarding. My personal conviction is that all the great spiritual traditions of the world have endured because they share certain basic truths and goals. Although my personal practice uses methodologies from specific traditions, I have no vested interest in their being any more effective than methodologies from other spiritual traditions.

The reader will notice that in all the cases presented in this book where I have recommended to patients that they practice a particular meditation technique or become acquainted with certain books, these are techniques and books that have been meaningful to me. I want to emphasize that I recommend these techniques because they are ones I know and use myself, and I present them in that context and with that explanation. I would certainly be entirely supportive of any exploration or practice a patient proposed from a spiritual tradition, if it were indeed one that seemed to have particular significance for that patient.

It is important to consider how the introduction of transpersonal material might alter the transference relationship, the fantasied relationship (recapitulating a childhood family relationship) that patients feel exists with the therapist. Psychotherapists trained in traditional psychodynamic theory may well wonder about the effects on the transference relationship of discussing personal spiritual issues and practices between therapist and patient. In classic tradition, the neutrality of the therapist was deemed crucial for the development of a transference relationship that could then be interpreted and worked through. My own belief, based on my experience and practice, is that true neutrality is really a hypothetical rather than an actual possibility. Patients deduce a great deal of personal information just by observing the therapist's mode of dressing, his or her choice of office decor, or the reading material on the bookshelf. It has been my experience that when a transference relationship promises to be the primary means through which a patient's area of difficulty will be revealed and worked through, this transference relationship will develop even if the patient knows a great deal about the therapist. Far from impeding the course of therapy, I feel that some awareness on the part of my patients of my own philosophical convictions has, in fact, a salutary effect on the working alliance—the mature level (as opposed to the transference level) of our therapist-patient relationship.

Although I hesitate to say anything to my patients that sounds like a dogmatic belief system, I do hold certain beliefs about the nature of human beings and our possibilities for growth and development. I believe, for instance, that all human beings have a certain inviolable essence that can be respected, regardless of their behavior. Furthermore, I believe that the universe (and all that exists within it) is one interrelated and interdependent whole. I feel that it is part of our inherent psychic organization to want to be in touch with our kinship and connectedness with everything else that exists. Not only do I find this to be the central drive that motivates us to embark on a spiritual search in our lives, but I also see it as the underpinning for a great deal of what we experience as psychological pain in our life.

A slightly different facet of the same issue is how I see human nature. In my early psychiatric training, I was taught that human nature had at its core dual drives—one showing as loving and one showing as negative (angry, hateful, destructive feelings and actions). I no longer feel that way. My studies of spirituality and my psychotherapeutic experiences have led me to feel that at our core we are loving, and that's our primary nature. Any time our lovingness is not visible, some fear system is occluding it. A way of imaging this would be to see our loving nature as the sun. During the day, the sun is always shining and is not visible only when clouds cover it. The clouds are our fear systems. We do not need to turn on the sun (our lovingness)—we need only clear away the clouds (fear systems). This might be a very simplified overview of what psychotherapy is attempting to do. Spiritual approaches have specific psychotherapeutic value when seen as being used to resolve our fear systems; they help us cultivate compassion, forgiveness, and acceptance and help us learn to temper our anger.

While holding this view, I see myself at the same time as working with patients on the problems they have with internal conflicts, such as guilt and fear and conflicts with family and friends and in work relationships. I see the value of viewing all these components of our small life's drama within the larger context of all of existence. I think this is a view that honors the potential of each individual. My patients, I believe, feel this as evidence that I esteem and respect them, and they respond to it positively.

Chapter 2

Introducing
Transpersonal Interventions

I IMAGINE THAT MANY THERAPISTS seeking to introduce the transpersonal into their therapy practice are doing so for the same reasons I did. As we begin to appreciate the important role existential issues play in our own lives, we cannot help but consider their presence or absence in the lives of the people we treat. As we explore and work with various spiritual disciplines or techniques, and as we find these techniques to be helpful to us, it makes sense that we would want to introduce them to our patients.

Within the framework of Self Psychology, I would like to examine, from a theoretical point of view, two main spiritual practices that I recommend to patients (Buddhism and *A Course in Miracles*), to isolate what I believe represents their major therapeutic components. I hope that as case material is presented later in the book, this framework will serve as a reference point for understanding how the introduction of spiritual practices affected the problems with which the patients presented themselves.

In considering the ways in which *A Course in Miracles* promotes change, we can review the ways in which healthy parent/child relations facilitate good ego development. According to the Self Psychologists, the mirroring function refers to that aspect of the baby's relationship with its parents in which the parents look at and mirror back to the baby its sense of pride and expansiveness, which later leads to a healthy sense of ambition and assertiveness. Using

Christian terminology, *A Course in Miracles* directly states that "in our essence" we are perfect and need only "awaken" to realize our wonderful, true, and sinless nature. According to the *Course*, the only "sin" is the illusory belief that we are separate entities. Daily meditations affirm this belief. When this is interpreted as "God loves me and thinks I am great," it can have a very positive healing function on a fragile and damaged sense of self. As will be discussed at length later, such a belief system may also have the undesirable effect of undermining an already fragile sense of self, such as might exist in psychotic persons. Much as one can play a musical instrument loudly or softly, the transpersonal therapist can emphasize certain aspects of the spiritual practice and de-emphasize others. Thus, a caveat: with patients whose sense of self is tenuous, I would play down the idea of being at one with God, i.e., without ego boundaries.

A Course in Miracles can fulfill the idealizing function, as described by the Self Psychologists. A student of the *Course* can have a healing idealizing transference. The term "idealizing transference" is used to denote the reactivation of aspects of the development of the self that were inadequate in the child's relationship with the significant parent. Working with the *Course*, individuals establish this relationship with Jesus or with the teachings themselves. It is possible to develop this relationship to the teachings, since they represent the teachings of a spiritually more advanced (and therefore more powerful, wise, and calm) being. The stated goal of the *Course* is the very desirable development of inner peace. It is easy, therefore, to see the teachings performing the role of a benevolent parent.

The alter ego or twinship function (as described by the Self Psychologists) of a healthy parent/child relationship can also be seen in *A Course in Miracles*. People who practice the *Course* see themselves as part of a special group who have chosen to follow this path. Although group practice is not obligatory, students of the *Course* often join study groups. There is a camaraderie, a sense of working together on a project (to become enlightened, to improve and help the world, etc.), a feeling of belonging—of being both teacher and student. (The *Course* emphasizes that everyone is both a teacher and a student at all times.) This type of collaboration can help one develop new and more positive interpersonal abilities. It can also be heartening on the long and arduous spiritual journey with all of its challenges, pitfalls, and discouragements.

Another significant therapeutic value of the *Course* is the emphasis it places on forgiveness of self and others, as revealed in its stance of non-aggression. This can be a very powerful tool in modifying lifelong habits and mental states because these newer approaches are being reinforced with daily meditations and affirmations.

Can we use the same approach for the Buddhist meditational path? I believe we can. In Buddhist practice in the West, the mirroring function of the parent/child relationship is often fulfilled by the meditation teachers. In the Buddhist tradition, it is believed that listening to the teachings of the Buddha is fortunate. To be in the position of a meditator at a retreat, therefore, affirms that one is a special person, one who has cultivated merit by developing traits needed on the way to Buddhahood. Ideally, the meditation teachers approach students in this respectful way. Unlike the *Course*, where it is possible to identify with the idea that "God loves me," there is no God in Buddhism. However, I suspect that a major mirroring occurs when I suggest to my patients that they begin Buddhist meditation under the aegis of a meditation teacher. I believe they feel this means that they are "worthy" of doing this practice. I often tell the people I work with that I see them as rough-cut diamonds with some debris in their consciousness, covering, in part, their inherent light and beauty, and our working together is to reveal to them their inherent "wonderfulness."

It is easy to discern how the idealizing function of relationship develops in Buddhist practice. Idealization of the Buddha and the subsequent teachers in this tradition is very strong. The Buddha is seen as wise, strong, compassionate, calm, forgiving, and, therefore, eminently "idealizeable." To a lesser degree, the teachers in this tradition, as well as respected teachers in all spiritual traditions, can also serve this function.

In Buddhism, the sangha, or community of like-minded spiritual companions, provides the camaraderie required for this idealizing function. In addition, there is an excitement to being part of a twenty-five-hundred-year-old tradition, to practicing meditation exactly as described by the Buddha. Completing a meditation retreat, overcoming the trials and tribulations of sitting for long periods of time while attempting to train the mind in a setting of silence, can provide a great sense of accomplishment which builds self-confidence.

In addition to the specific beneficial relational functions that may be shown to be operative in spiritual practice, I believe there is yet another dimension which is greater than the sum of the parts. There is an indescribable, almost mysterious, excitement about starting a path that seeks to probe humankind's deepest questions: "Who are we? Is there a big picture? If the answer is yes, where or how do we fit in? What is our role in life? Is there some greater purpose to our lives?" I believe these are the essential core dilemmas with which we all struggle, and I feel patients building a real rapport with me and a conviction that I understand their situation when I address these issues as if they lie within the valid domain of psychotherapy.

I would like to make a few general comments regarding the similarities of certain aspects of Buddhist practice and *A Course in Miracles*. The goal of both practices is equanimity or inner peace. Both provide meditations that can produce states of joy and calm. In the Theravadan Buddhist tradition, Vipassana or mindfulness meditation is considered to be the major practice leading to liberation or enlightenment. The success of this practice can result in a diminished sense of a separate, enduring self and in the awareness of the non-permanence of everything we perceive. This may lead to a lessening of anxiety regarding loss. *A Course in Miracles* uses both cognitive and contemplative meditations to achieve the same ends.

An interesting and more recent derivative of Heinz Kohut's Self Psychology is the development of the intersubjective approach as a method to expand our way of understanding and treating psychological problems. Although this is not Stolorow *et al*'s main point, it's significant because I think this is the first time in traditional (Freudian) psychoanalytic circles that there has been a move away from the more rigid and dualistic model of the isolated individual mind toward a view in which there is a "softening" of boundaries and a greater focus on the field existing between, for example, the therapist and patient. In spiritual practice, an often-stated goal is the "softening" of boundaries to such an extent as to render them nonexistent. Purportedly, certain saints and holy people not only could empathize with the pain of others, but "eliminated" their boundaries completely so that they could actually experience others' pain.

I believe that the basis of all fear is our attachment to our boundaries. Our DNA or biology (see information re limbic systems and reptilian brain in Chapter 9) focuses greatly on the survival of this "separate" self we call ourselves. The lessening or elimination of our attachment to this separate sense of ourselves—*in a balanced way*—with full and healthy integration of this consciousness would therefore lead to states of non-fear and increased lovingness. Jack Engler speaks of the need to become "somebody" before becoming "nobody" (p. 24, his book with Wilber)—which means developing a mature ego, a healthy, balanced, strong, and integrated sense of separate self, before doing the work of lessening one's attachment to it.

In Ken Wilber's latest book *A Brief History of Everything,* he sums it up this way: "If you don't befriend Freud, it will be harder to get to Buddha." (155) I interpret his words to mean that "Freud" is representative of the early, infantile unconscious, neurotic traits that need to be resolved, while "Buddha" stands for the transcendental aspects of our spiritual search.

Many individuals without a healthy, strong ego (e.g., those who are considered psychotic, borderline, neurotic, and narcissistic) do indeed have genuine spiritual experiences. The difficulty here is that they are unable to integrate them into their lives to help them become more loving, wiser, etc. I strongly believe that whatever true spiritual insights one experiences will be expressed through the highest level of integration the person has. If there are lacunae (holes in the ego) of a psychotic, neurotic, or narcissistic nature, then there is a risk that the spiritual insights will be expressed through these lacunae. I believe this is what happens when spiritual teachers use their disciples for their own psychotic, neurotic, or narcissistic needs.

The Stolorow *et al* writings are helpful also in that they continue to emphasize and focus on the relational (intersubjective) aspects of our lives. All too often, we see individuals on a "spiritual path" who are so eager to find "God" or become "enlightened" that they forget, minimize, misuse, or even abuse the relational aspect of their lives. In the Zen tradition, as exemplified by the Ten Ox Herder Pictures, even after enlightenment one goes back to one's village to help others. The same is true for the saint, bodhisattva, or tzaddick. (A comprehensive study of the Ten Ox Herder Pictures is found in Lex Hixon's book, *Coming Home.*)

In their zeal to incorporate transpersonal techniques, therapists need to bear in mind that although transpersonal techniques may be useful for a wide spectrum of levels of psychological development, the hoped-for goal in the application of each of these techniques will differ according to each patient's level of psychodynamic development. Transpersonal techniques, by which I mean the study and practice of techniques that derive from spiritual traditions, have as their general goal the transcendence of the personal ego (the sense of separate self) and the development of unity consciousness. We need, therefore, to analyze how these techniques are helpful for people at varying levels of psychological development.

The case studies presented in this book demonstrate how the various spiritual techniques may be used to good advantage with a variety of patients. I have divided these case studies into seven general areas. The first of these areas will describe the use of transpersonal techniques with people with psychotic illness. The most fundamental understanding of the psychoses is that they reflect a basic flaw in ego development, probably the result of a genetic anomaly of the perceptual apparatus affecting psychological development from the time of an individual's birth. The wide range of maladaptive symptoms that make up the various psychoses all reflect, to some degree, the individual's inability to interpret correctly his or her thoughts and feelings and to acknowledge them as originating within him- or herself rather than in others. This is often referred to as "defect in ego boundaries" or "undifferentiated ego boundaries." Based on this basic misperception, such people often have problems correctly evaluating a situation and making realistic life plans. Their poor judgment frequently makes it difficult for them to be successful in a worldly sense, and often their difficulties are compounded by feelings of low self-esteem.

One might appropriately conclude that the practice of a meditation technique that promotes the dissolution of ego boundaries would be a poor choice for an individual who is already struggling with undifferentiated ego boundaries. Likewise, silent meditation retreats where one is left alone for hours (or days) with no external reference or support for one's inner thoughts and perceptions would also be a poor choice for people in this category. However, short daily periods of structured meditation, such as the use of a mantra (particularly if the word or phrase is a soothing or reassuring one), may have a calming effect and prove to be beneficial.

I frequently recommend the study of *A Course in Miracles* for severely emotionally disturbed persons, particularly if their illness includes a great deal of anger and rage. Although the *Course* is actually a very sophisticated tool for working toward the transcendence of individual ego boundaries, its familiar Christian terminology and its respect for each individual being seem to be very soothing and reassuring to severely disturbed people. I also find that recommending certain transpersonal reading materials is particularly helpful with severely disturbed patients. There are two ways in which this may be understood. First, with severely disturbed people who have poor self-esteem, I think the idea that I am recommending reading material to them that I have personally found to be helpful builds their own ego strength through identification with me. They feel empowered by their perception that I find them capable of doing spiritual work. People with psychotic illness often over-idealize the therapist. Second, I emphasize kindness and forgiveness, especially with psychotic patients, and I sometimes think these patients overestimate my capacity to be kind, my capacity to forgive, as well as my skill in meditation. While I certainly am careful not to misrepresent myself in any way, I think this over-idealization of the therapist may actually be helpful. For individuals with a poor level of ego development, an over-idealized yet genuinely caring, empathic, and consistent therapist may be the most therapeutic tool.

Some of the case histories presented in the chapter on the borderline psychotic patient will reflect other ways in which transpersonal reading material may be helpful. Borderline patients often have obsessive or rigid belief systems with hyperrage occurring frequently. Even though these belief systems usually are painful, it is difficult for these people to entertain or maintain other perspectives of reality. Current psychological researchers now theorize that there may be a biological and/or genetic component involved. It often happens, however, that after a long period of working with me and intuiting some aspects of my own world view, their attachment to their belief systems and ways of operating begins to soften. It has been my experience that suggesting reading material by a famous author, thinker, or spiritual teacher frequently promotes dramatic changes in a short time. If I were to mention to patients *my* beliefs or *my* views, this might be construed as a challenge to, or in some way a criticism of, their beliefs. It might be perceived as a threat. When I suggest to patients that I have found the thoughts or teachings of some famous person helpful, they can feel more free to be open to the material. Also, this is again a situation of sharing something important of my own with a patient, a gesture that patients at all levels of psychological development appreciate.

I have included two individuals who had suffered classic mood disorder illness—one for most of his adult life, the other having developed his illness in mid-life. Both, moreover, had been spiritual seekers most of their adult lives, so no introduction to spiritual issues was necessary. They already had established study, meditation, and prayer practices.

What my transpersonal orientation helped with here was my ability to be truly empathic with the positive spiritual experiences they were having during the psychotic phases of their illnesses, while keeping the focus of the therapy on their non-functioning in their everyday lives. Following the psychotic episodes, a transpersonal approach could help the patients to begin to integrate some of their more positive experiences into their everyday lives. As I discuss further in the chapter, this work would have been almost impossible without the biochemical aid of anti-psychotic and anti-manic depressive medication.

The problems of pre-neurotic patients are usually related to traumas in the first few years of life. As I show in the clinical studies in that chapter, pre-neurotic patients usually have problems of low self-esteem and narcissism. Entitlement problems, too, frequently stem from traumas during this early period in life. Bearing that in mind, I have noted considerable lessening of symptoms when patients in this category were introduced to meditation practice. I believe the practice itself and the tranquil setting of meditation retreats provide some of the healing nurturance these individuals require. On another front, the theme of forgiveness, as emphasized in *A Course in Miracles*, is a tool that I have used successfully to bolster self-esteem. An often-quoted truism in spiritual circles is that the price of freedom is forgiveness. Or, to put it another way, the mind state of non-forgiveness implies an attachment to events of the past. Traditional psychotherapy tries to help us "let go" or come to terms with the past. Some of these spiritual tools, especially those that involve the practice of forgiveness, greatly speed up this healing process. *A Course in Miracles* emphasizes universal acceptance in the teachings and stresses the preciousness of each individual—concepts pre-neurotic patients often find soothing and healing.

In the chapter on working with people with neurotic illness, I point out how various types of meditation practice are specifically helpful in bringing to consciousness previously repressed conflictual material. A classical way of understanding neuroses is that they are unresolved conflicts centering around misperceptions, fears, or traumas involving members of one's nuclear family during the first years of life. A person who might be diagnosed as neurotic would be understood to have a fairly well consolidated ego. This would include the presence of a conscience, the ability to feel and put off gratification of one's impulses, and the capacity to control the conflict between impulse and conscience. The presence of neurotic illness presupposes that an individual is able to differentiate between self and other, and that he or she has developed sufficient mechanisms for keeping impulses within socially acceptable bounds. Neurotic symptoms (e.g., inhibitions, guilt) are often characterized as the ego's compromise expression of instinctual drive inhibited by the constraints of conscience.

The anxiety that so often characterizes neurotic illness and the lack of self-awareness of the genesis of one's problems are two symptoms of neurosis that are often, in my experience, helped by meditation practice. Concentration practices, fixing the attention on a single object (word, mantra, inner sound, inner vision, a particular body sensation such as breathing), have both a physiologically and an emotionally calming effect. As a person's anxiety level is reduced, his or her ability to be introspective and to tolerate the reemergence of repressed (often frightening) material increases.

In addition, I believe the case material in the chapter on the treatment of neuroses most clearly shows the potential of awareness meditation, such as Vipassana, for uncovering unconscious psychological material. Patients who have begun this practice have often reported to me that they have uncovered and reexperienced in meditation "forgotten" incidents that had never emerged in their therapy sessions or even in their dreams. (This is especially true of those people who have practiced in the context of intensive meditation retreats.) They always commented that the baseline of calm that is established through consistent practice was a steadying enough factor to allow them to recall and reexperience, with affect, repressed events from their distant past. This has been my own experience with the practice as well. At this level of psychological functioning, Vipassana practice bears considerable similarity to the technique of free association in psychoanalysis.

The next chapter of case studies reflects the level at which transpersonal practices are helpful to people at a post-neurotic, existential level of psychological functioning. At this stage, a spiritual teacher or guide might be as valuable as a therapist. This is, I believe, the level at which spiritual tools were meant to be used. However, it has been my clinical experience that even for people with highly developed, well-functioning egos who approach spiritual practice as a tool for transcendence, there usually remains some residue of unresolved conflicts at lower levels of psychosexual development. It is my belief that, as these conflicts are resolved, more energy is available to an individual for continued spiritual growth. It has also been my clinical impression that people with well-integrated, well-functioning egos who seek psychotherapy for reasons of existential angst usually have issues of midlife psychology to be worked on in therapy and are therefore excellent prospects for beginning spiritual work.

The case of Marian presents an example of the effects of spiritual practice on an individual who had completed a course of psychotherapy that had been considered "successful." Although this person had worked diligently in psychotherapy, certain habitual fears and patterns of behavior had remained present. These discomforting "mind habits" began to disappear after some degree of "awakening" occurred with mindfulness meditation, and their lessening appeared to be directly related to the insights arising from the meditation. It seemed clear to me that the traditional psychological therapies had been insufficient to accomplish some final resolutions.

I felt it important to include a chapter on relationships. By working on the healing of relationships we can actually work on the impediments that keep us from unity consciousness (being at one with the divine, Godhead, emptiness, nothingness, everythingness, etc.).

Significant work on the midbrain by Dr. Joseph LeDoux helps us focus on the genetic, biochemical derivatives of our anger, which, although initially evolved for purposes of our physical survival, nevertheless can get in the way of our emotional survival, especially with loved ones in a relationship.

In my 1980 paper, "Anger and the Fear of Death," the data was already there pointing to this. It is the same fear that our egos have when it comes to letting go of our life-long beliefs and ways of looking at the world that involve the lessening of (or death of) the ego.

I show how working with couples can access this very rapidly by getting to the fear behind the anger or negativity in the relationship. A specific technique is demonstrated for getting behind our neocortical (higher brain) way of thinking and accessing the fear that stems from the midbrain that sets into motion the (physical survival) anger that we think we'll need to survive.

Approaches borrowed from spiritual traditions are explained, and it is shown how they can strengthen our higher brain functions (neocortical) to override unnecessary negativity or anger and/or dampen the quality and quantity of the anger "pushed" by our midbrain (limbic) system.

The introduction of a transpersonal dimension into traditional psychotherapy has the potential of being beneficial at all levels of psychosexual development, yet it also presents the need for caution in certain areas. At the more severely disturbed end of the spectrum of psychological development, vigilance needs to be maintained that a patient not misconstrue the notion that there is only one consciousness of which we are all a part. On the level of metaphysical reality we may understand this to be the fundamental spiritual truth. On the level of day-to-day reality it is important, especially for psychotic individuals, to understand that they are not magically connected to all other beings. While it is indeed true that some very skilled meditators, in the course of their meditation practice, develop apparently paranormal powers, it is important for psychotic individuals not to overvalue the power of their thoughts.

Another caveat to therapists seeking to introduce a transpersonal dimension into their work is the potential risk that patients will use their evaluation of the therapist's spirituality to heighten their dependency. As I pointed out earlier, some over-idealization of the therapist, followed by identification with him or her, seems to be therapeutic. However, especially when working with people with a sense of self that is poorly consolidated, the therapist needs to be careful about the amount of guidance and direction provided. In our enthusiasm to share what has been helpful for us, we may inadvertently contribute to certain patients' feelings of dependency.

A final caution about the introduction of the transpersonal seems in order. At all levels of the spectrum of psychosexual development, it seems possible to use "the spiritual path" as a way to avoid dealing with uncomfortable situations in daily life. High levels of meditation achievement and insight do not necessarily guarantee that one's impulses will be well controlled and appropriately gratified, that one's interpersonal relationships will be satisfying, that one can work and contribute in a meaningful way in one's community. It seems to me that we need to do our spiritual work at the same time that we work out our intrapsychic and interpersonal conflicts. I try to be alert in my practice to point out to patients when they seem to be using their time of meditation to avoid resolving family conflicts.

I often advise a person in a relationship that is just in its formative stages against leaving to do an extended meditation retreat. In fact, I try as much as possible to point out how a relationship and the family seem to provide just as fertile ground for working on awareness, compassion, and forgiveness as a meditation retreat.

While it is possible to use meditation to avoid feelings, it is possible for people conversant in transpersonal psychological theory to use this theory to gloss over or avoid feelings that are uncomfortable for them. For example, a person wanting to avoid experiencing the grief associated with the loss of a love relationship may talk philosophically about an awareness of impermanence in the universe. I try to be alert for these shifts toward philosophical discourse and, although I believe the content of the discourse to be essentially true, encourage my patients to stay with a discussion of their feelings and to experience these feelings as fully as they can. For those of my patients with enough psychological sophistication to be able to recognize and work with this defensive maneuver, it is helpful. We—these patients and I—then stay alert for each instance in which our interchange shifts from the acknowledgment of current affect into philosophical discourse, and we try to recognize what emerging feeling this shift in affect level was designed to avoid.

I applaud the trend in psychotherapy, spearheaded by the Humanistic Psychology movement, that encourages us to see patients in larger terms than simple diagnostic labels. However, for the purposes of this book, I do feel it is important to separate the case histories into various diagnostic categories. If we are to function successfully as therapists, transpersonal or otherwise, we must recognize that diagnostic labels are a shortcut to understanding the specific level of psychosexual development from which a person's current difficulties stem.

Lack of such a careful diagnostic formulation may be of particular significance to transpersonal psychotherapists. One way of defining transpersonal psychotherapy is by the content of the material produced by the patient. For example, some patients seek therapy because they have been frightened or overwhelmed by extraordinary experiences which they assess as "spiritual." These experiences might include feelings of being dissociated from their body, an alteration of visual or auditory perceptions, or a sense of dissolution of ego boundaries. Since all of these phenomena can occur in meditation, we might mistakenly assume that a person experiencing them is basically psychologically intact. All of these experiences can also reflect primitive strata of psychological organization, and so it is very important for transpersonal therapists to take a careful psychodynamic history to make sure that they are looking at a complete picture of the patient's functioning.

Ken Wilber, in his paper "The Pre/Trans Fallacy," cautions therapists about the need to discriminate between "transpersonal phenomena" that reflect an immature level of ego organization and these same phenomena as a manifestation of mature psychospiritual development. I have made this error myself, particularly with pre-neurotic disorders when they manifest in people who seem to function fairly well. My sense is that probably I was particularly pleased to note the emergence of "transpersonal material," and my eagerness to talk about these matters may have obscured my ability to recognize at first more severe underlying psychopathology.

As we proceed into the case studies themselves, I would like to make some general remarks about the question of how one might introduce transpersonal or spiritual issues into an otherwise traditional practice. The "ethics" of doing this has never created a problem for me. As I mentioned earlier, I do take a careful history when I begin to work with patients about what their religious background was and what their current relationship is to spiritual practice. When this dimension is present in someone's life, and when its presence has been a positive one, I do everything I can to reinforce it. To the degree that I am conversant with a person's own spiritual tradition, I try to look for meditation techniques within that tradition when recommending meditation as a discipline. If I know the tradition well enough, I try to use its teachings, philosophies, and stories to support issues in psychotherapy.

When I share the spiritual practices that I do myself or suggest to patients that they try them, I am very sensitive to the particular weight that any suggestion from me might have, in terms either of transference or even the normally inflated esteem in which therapists are often held by their patients. I am, therefore, very sensitive about not appearing too eager or too determined to have my patients follow my suggestions. If a patient does not respond to my tentative reference to matters transpersonal, such as when I suggest reading material or meditation practice, I continue quite traditionally. Even though I think that the addition of the transpersonal dimension enhances a traditional psychotherapy practice, I very much respect the degree of help the traditional therapy alone can provide. For many people, for a variety of reasons, the introduction of the transpersonal is inappropriate and might even have a negative effect.

Ultimately, I do not think there can be a guidebook to the "how" and "when" to introduce the transpersonal. This is consistent with my feeling that good psychotherapy, while definitely based on certain scientific formulations, is essentially an art. Regardless of how much we know about either the biology or the psychodynamics of psychological functioning, effective psychotherapy reflects empathy, intuition, skill, and sensitivity on the part of the therapist, a good working alliance, and a firm sense of commitment between the therapist and patient.

Transference, Countertransference, and the Working Alliance

The basic issue under consideration in this book is the addition of spiritual practices such as meditation or spiritual studies to traditional psychodynamic psychotherapy. Because this clearly requires the revealing of the therapist's belief system, often of the therapist's values, it is important to address the issues of "anonymity" of the therapist, or therapist "neutrality." Both of these notions, part of conventional psychiatric wisdom, need to be understood in terms of their effect on transference and countertransference. What I hope to clarify is that an apparent positive regard on the part of the therapist toward the patient is more than appropriate—it is the fundamental ingredient of the working alliance, the commitment that patient and therapist make to each other to examine honestly their relationship as it unfolds so that unconscious unresolved issues can be brought to consciousness and healed.

A concern has been raised that by introducing a transpersonal dimension to the therapy (such as suggesting that a patient study a particular meditation) I destroy my anonymity. I do. In 1987, I wrote an article for *Common Boundary* in which I expressed my ideas about revealing to patients my interest in the spiritual component of my life and why and how this area might be of help to them. One of the respondents was critical of my breach of the anonymity stance of the therapist. Since then, this matter seems to be undergoing revision, with many senior training psychoanalysts openly taking the view that going beyond neutrality and sharing the derivatives of the therapist's inner self can advance the process of treatment and may be essential for successful treatment. In an article in *Psychiatric Times* entitled "Self-Disclosure: A Two-Level Issue," Dr. Arnold L. Gilberg cites Atwood, Brandschaft, Hoffman, Natterson, Renick, Schwaber, Stolorow, and himself as psychoanalysts whose viewpoints support the therapist's use of self-revelation as part of the therapeutic process. I strongly feel that the introduction of spiritual issues into the therapist-patient arena fits the area these psychoanalysts are addressing.

Working with transference has been a cornerstone of the psychodynamic therapeutic process. Transference is the unconscious attribution by the patient to the therapist of mind states, opinions, or views that were held by significant people in the patient's own early life. Transference makes sense. The expectation that all people will react to us as our family did is quite reasonable. Children of highly critical parents are apt to imagine that people are judging them, and people whose parents applauded them most likely expect that they will be well received. Sometimes transference assumptions are strong enough to significantly impair people's ability to feel good about themselves, to make decisive life choices, and to work out those difficulties of a relationship that actually are present rather than those they *imagine* are present. Psychodynamic, interpretive psychotherapy is particularly helpful in correcting transference distortions. A skilled therapist, as part of the therapeutic contract with the patient, will be able, empathically, to help the patient discover the ways in which he or she unconsciously continues to be bound by (and victimized by) the relationships of childhood.

It used to be a widely held belief that the "transference neurosis," the establishment of a relationship with the therapist that mimics the dynamics of one's childhood, could happen only if the therapist remained strictly anonymous. No personal clue about the therapist was deemed appropriate, and gestures of common courtesy such as a welcoming handshake were taboo.

Although this seemed to be the theoretically expressed view, the role models in my early training all seemed openly warm and empathic. My models included Ralph Greenson, Michael Balint, Donald Winnicott, and Otto Fleishman, who, as I listened to them describe their work with patients, gave the impression that their patients really knew that their therapists cared for them. In 1956, I was a resident in Psychiatry at The Menninger Clinic in Topeka, Kansas. Dr. Otto Fleishman, then director of the Psychoanalytic Institute, would see patients in psychotherapy while residents observed the process through a one-way view mirror. (The patients knew that they were being observed.) We followed one particular patient, a young and beautiful woman, through a course of twice-a-week therapy for three years. All the aspects of a classical oedipal neurosis arose in the transference, were explored, and were seemingly satisfactorily resolved. This included her attributing to Dr. Fleishman feelings, desires, and opinions that were reconstructions of her childhood. Also, Dr. Fleishman was not particularly anonymous. In addition to her sitting and facing him (as opposed to the conventional lying-on-the-couch style of therapy), he often smiled at her warmly. On one occasion, we asked him why he had said something to her that seemed friendly. He replied, "Because I like her!" He described how, in Vienna, where heating systems were poor, analysts would often cover patients with a blanket to keep them warm. Furthermore, patients were always greeted with a handshake, considered proper manners at the time. It was clear from studying with Dr. Fleishman that behaving like a responsive and responsible human being did not interfere with the emergence of a transference neurosis and its resolution. Indeed, remaining remote and aloof might have resulted in missing important clues.

My own experience has shown me that my openness about my positive regard for my patients is itself a valuable tool for exploring their feelings. Often, especially when I am feeling relaxed and attentive, I smile at my patients. Depending on a person's difficulties, he or she might interpret my smiling as kindness, benevolence, or, at the other extreme, as mockery. My skill at being able to elicit their reaction to whatever my behavior is (smiling or not smiling, speaking a lot or listening quietly) is what interpretive psychotherapy is all about. Rather than being some unwanted, situation-confusing event, transference revealed is the key to reconstructing, patient and therapist together, the world view of the patient's childhood, which continues to shape the response patterns of the patient's adult life.

Transference reactions on the part of the patient, brought clearly into perspective with the help of the therapist, are obviously useful. What is necessary is that the therapist be continuously alert to his or her own transference reactions. Pitfalls in therapy occur when transference and countertransference reactions operate unheeded on the part of the therapist toward the patient. Therapists run the same risk as anyone else of viewing another person as their own mother, father, sibling, or child. Psychologically sophisticated people have sometimes mentioned to me that they sought me as a therapist because they knew that they had issues with their father to resolve and I fit the role of an "older man." In fact, one does not need a specific therapist image in order for transference to operate. Transference is always operating. Whatever our strongest disabling entanglements are, they will emerge in transference responses toward those with whom we are intimately involved.

Dr. Fleishman's young patient responded to him in a girlish, seductive manner, convinced that he was a handsome man romantically drawn to her when, manifestly, he was a small, elderly grandfather—benevolent, perhaps, but not in sexual pursuit. For Dr. Fleishman to respond to her perceptions as if they were valid, or, especially, to solicit these reactions by behaving seductively, would have been countertransference. Countertransference (a word often confused and misused) may perhaps be most succinctly defined as the unconscious assumption of the projected perception of the patient so as to actually recreate the conflictual relationship of the patient's childhood. Clearly, at best this only exacerbates the painful struggle that brought the patient to therapy in the first place. At worst, it leads to inappropriate therapist-patient relationships (often including sexual expression) that are, unfortunately, not rare enough. The only remedy for this, in addition to impeccable professional integrity, is constant monitoring on the part of the therapist of his or her own emotional responses to the ever-shifting climate of the intimate psychotherapeutic relationship.

Transference on the part of the therapist means projecting onto the patient the views or expectations of the therapist's significant models, parents, or siblings. The same potentially dire sequelae may arise as a result of unheeded transference as in the event of unheeded countertransference. At best, the therapist continues his or her own unresolved struggles at the expense (literally) of the patient, and the patient does not improve. At worst, therapists may involve patients in coerced intimate relationships or abandon them, leaving them even more severely disturbed. Both of these outcomes are sadly cruel.

Transference and countertransference on the part of the therapist (responses that can be pitfalls if not consciously monitored and judiciously handled) have nothing to do with warm, benevolent feelings of positive regard. Liking someone and genuinely wishing for his or her well-being is *not* transference. Joseph Natterson, in his excellent book *Beyond Countertransference*, clearly states that the therapist's caring feelings toward the patient are indispensable for the therapeutic process and have at least as important a status as interpretations. He describes the loving and caring feelings he experiences toward his patients and the ways in which he lets them know about those feelings.

Natterson, in his work, is continuing the tradition of Heinz Kohut in emphasizing the shift of the role of the therapist from that of someone with a professional function to that of a human being with personal feelings. In the tradition of Self Psychology taught by Kohut, the crucial ingredient in healing is empathy. Just interpreting *how* and *why* people develop the fears, inhibitions, and limitations they currently struggle with is seen as unfeeling as well as unhelpful. Rather, the therapist needs to be able to *convey* to patients a felt sense of empathy with their pain as it continues to manifest in their current lives, much as it did earlier in their lives when empathic parental support should have been present but wasn't.

Empathy does not happen in a vacuum. It is our natural response to people we care about, whose pain and joy we feel as our own. How bizarre it is to pretend that we feel neutral toward our patients. In fact, it seems self-evident that people who select the healing arts as a profession are those who began with warm regard for all persons and a desire to ease pain.

In a paper delivered to the San Francisco Psychoanalytic Society (February 12, 1996), Dr. Samuel Gershon, a psychoanalyst, wrestles with the issue of neutrality in the psychotherapeutic situation ("Neutrality, Resistance and Self-Disclosure in an Intersubjective Psychoanalysis").

Coming from the position of the psychoanalytic intersubjective model, Gershon posits that rather than seeing "neutrality" in the older and more traditional way as a type of opaque screen behind which the therapist hides his or her thoughts, feelings, etc., "neutrality first makes its appearance as a moment of new appreciation of the other . . . [and] is rapidly threatened by the encroachments of the surrounding transference/countertransference configurations. Yet in each moment of neutrality a degree of mutual recognition and trust is established and becomes an available haven, one which may be found again in the midst of a repetitive engagement in a transference/countertransference scenario."

Later, Gershon says, "Neutrality is best thought of as a mutual achievement of patient and analyst . . . which is the very purpose of psychoanalysis and which, therefore, *cannot be its precondition*" (Italics mine.). This definition may be the cutting edge toward which pyschoanalysis is moving. I would like to suggest that the area of spirituality and its insights not contaminated with the vicissitudes of transference/countertransference could be considered as one of those havens where the therapist and the patient can see themselves and each other in a new light.

If the fundamental message is that we are all parts of the one cosmos, Godhead, consciousness, etc., then that realization can lead to the eventual equality (and neutrality) of two human beings struggling to find their oneness. Our hand putting food in our mouth doesn't see itself as being kindly or compassionate; rather, it is just the natural order of cooperativeness. In the same vein, seen from the spiritual perspective, the patient and therapist can have as a goal a mutual (intersubjective) appreciation of their basic oneness and equalness. Gershon points to the intersubjective resistances that both patient and therapist encounter, which, I believe, we need to struggle with in the area of this profound spiritual insight.

I think that when the needs of the patient dictate that there be no conscious spiritual dimension to the psychotherapy, the therapist working on his or her own resistances to the above realization will ultimately help the patient. Thus, in some way, this becomes a type of couples or relationship therapy, where, hopefully, the therapist has fewer problems to distort the relationship.

Because the transference/countertransference relationship can distort anything, obviously if and when a spiritual dimension is added to the therapy, the therapist needs to be vigilant that this too is an arena to be carefully monitored. If we use the intersubjective field model, the patient will "help" us notice when true neutrality is lost, because we will then *not* see each other as we really are. The patient usually in some way calls our attention, if we don't notice it first, to some countertransference action on our part. Not only can this help the therapy, but it can ultimately help the therapist and patient with their spiritual quests. For example, the therapist might see the therapeutic situation as a hierarchical arrangement of power and privilege whose purpose is to maintain a position of authoritative objectivity and omniscience. This may be an expression of the therapist's unconscious self-idealization.

It is not uncommon for the therapist to have loving feelings (non-erotic) in the interaction which will certainly prevent burnout and can be experienced somehow by the patient as a very profound caring.

Although I write more specifically about transference and countertransference issues as I describe my work with individual patients, there are some general concluding remarks that I want to make here.

I feel that it is crucial for students of transpersonal psychotherapy to learn one system well and depend on the skillful use of that psychological approach in dealing with patients. Therapists will study and explore various other disciplines and perhaps accumulate a "potpourri of spiritual techniques." Those techniques then become significant *adjuncts* to the therapy. It is imperative, I believe, that all transpersonal psychotherapists have a strong theoretical and practical psychological foundation to buttress and support their work.

I hope that by describing Dr. Fleishman's work I have shown that exhibiting caring does not matter in terms of the development of the transference distortions. In addition, the perceptions patients may have about me—that I like them enough to want the best for them, that I esteem them enough to share with them what is important to me, that I really care that they feel better—are *true*. This is not a transference distortion. With no equivocation, I believe that this all gives a great boost to the patient's morale in undertaking the difficult task of psychotherapeutic self-exploration.

Another possible criticism and valid concern about the therapist's adopting an attitude of open, positive, warm regard for the patient is that this might preclude the possibility of the patient's accessing negative feelings toward the therapist as a way of exploring inhibitions about negative feelings toward others in his or her life. I have not found this to be a difficulty in practice. For people who need to explore, express, and come to terms with negative feelings, my friendly attitude or pleasant smile will appear mocking, condescending, or ingenuous. My skill as a therapist rests in being able to stay alert to, elicit, and explore these perceptions without refuting them or feeling personally rebuked.

A final consideration that is appropriate here has to do with the difficult question, which faces all therapists, of how to continue to like, or at least to have positive regard for, patients who are not particularly endearing. It is hard to feel warm toward bigots, or toward people who cause alarm by threatening suicide, or people who critique (negatively) one's best therapeutic efforts. By contrast, one feels much more spontaneously pleased by patients who share one's values, "work hard" at therapy, and applaud one's efforts.

It is in the realm of maintaining genuine positive regard toward unendearing patients that my own personal spiritual practice has been most valuable. As long as I can feel that my patients are not separate from me, are not people who are "sick" whom I am trying to "cure," but, like me, are part of all humanity struggling for happiness, I can treat them with the same compassion I might feel toward my own arm if I broke it. When I recognize my own fundamental desire for happiness and see the mistakes I have made (and continue to make) in its pursuit, I can be more compassionate about the maladaptive efforts of others to reach happiness. When my own spiritual practice keeps me focused on the awesome reality of how mysterious life is—just in the fact that it is happening—I am exhilarated. My own shift from a personal stance of being a victim of an abusive mother, a difficult childhood, and of life in general, to becoming a grateful participant in the process of life itself inspires me with enthusiasm and energy. I generally feel excited and happy at the end of a long working day. This shift, perhaps partially a result of a fortunately happy adult family life, but most certainly primarily shaped by my spiritual perspective, has rewarded me with incredible relief and happiness. Because of this, the worse the pain I feel a person to be in, even if (and perhaps *especially* if) this pain manifests in unpleasantness, the more compassion I feel for him or her. It makes it easier to help the patient as I might help a wounded person struggling in pain, and I am moved to respond. As I wrote this last sentence, I thought perhaps I was now sounding like a religious zealot. I hope I sound like a good transpersonal psychotherapist.

Chapter 3

The Transpersonal Treatment of
Psychotic Disorders

THE CURRENTLY ACCEPTED TREATMENT of psychotic disorders involves supportive psychotherapy augmented by the use of phenothiazines. (For the non-physician reader: "phenothiazines" are the category of tranquilizers specifically effective in suppressing bizarre and irrational thinking.) Supportive psychotherapy usually involves helping patients function in their day-to-day activity and avoids the often stressful sequelae of interpretive psychotherapy focusing on early life experiences. I basically agree with this methodology. My primary goal in working with very disturbed individuals is to enable them to live their daily lives in as functional and gratifying a way as possible. Because individuals with this type of illness often struggle with unrealistic or even irrational thought patterns, I am cautious about the introduction of the transpersonal as this often involves abstract thinking about supermundane realities. However, it has been my experience that the judicious addition of certain transpersonal practices, both as a stabilizer of thinking and behavior and as a means of reducing excessive rage, is possible and practical.

My understanding of the etiology and dynamics of psychotic illness accords with current psychiatric views. That is, psychotic illness seems to represent a basic flaw in ego development, based on a defective genetic physiologic condition and a possible defective psychological environment, which makes it difficult for individuals to clearly recognize themselves as separate from others and/or maintain reasonable and rational thought processes. Some, but not all, individuals with psychotic illness struggle with excessive amounts of anger which, due to poorly differentiated ego boundaries, is often projected onto others and experienced as threatening and frightening.

While identification and diagnosis of psychotic individuals has been fairly consistent throughout the history of modern psychiatry, the understanding of its etiology has shifted in emphasis during the last two decades. Earlier psychiatric thinking emphasized the role of the family in producing psychotic illness in one of its members. Erik Erikson, René Spitz, and Margaret Mahler emphasized the significance of consistent and satisfactory nurturance of infants, especially in the first year of life. More recent psychiatric thinking stresses the existence of a basic, genetic flaw which makes it impossible for certain individuals to consolidate a differentiated, strong ego, quite apart from whatever the particular family dynamics may have been.

My own view is that *both* family and genetic factors play a significant role. I believe the fact that phenothiazine medication often entirely erases bizarre and disorderly thinking provides proof that this kind of thinking is biochemically related. The fact that research studies show the percentage of the population afflicted with psychotic illness is fairly consistent worldwide further supports the biochemical anomaly thesis.

I also believe that, in addition to biochemical predispositions, the role of the family in the development of a person with psychotic illness is significant. Because a major developmental problem for people with psychotic illness is the discrimination between self and others and the development of orderly thought processes, it would be most beneficial for potentially psychotic individuals to grow up in a family that is kindly and rational, as well as one in which limits and boundaries are clearly set. Because normal internal ego structure is lacking, benevolent external structure and support are helpful.

Supportive psychotherapy is the accepted adjunct to phenothiazine therapy. In supportive psychotherapy, the therapist becomes the auxiliary ego for the patient, helping him or her make life plans more consistent with rational and reasonable thinking.

Day-to-day problem solving is often the focus of this type of therapy. In these cases, the therapist models for the patient how sequential and thoughtful planning can be applied to life situations so that subsequent experience might unfold with some degree of comfort and gratification. Especially for those patients whose personal family background has been chaotic and ungratifying, the consistent support of a stable, thoughtful, reasonable therapist as an alter ego seems to offer the most help.

The addition of the transpersonal into the therapy of psychotic individuals is a sensitive issue. A primary goal for myself, in my own spiritual work, is the experience of unity consciousness, the awareness of interrelatedness with all beings. Working with patients whose principal difficulty is the development and discrimination of personal ego boundaries, I would hesitate to introduce notions of unity consciousness, but rather would emphasize the concept of the specialness and sanctity of every human being.

In Western religious practice, emphasis is placed on the uniqueness of each soul. Hindu practice includes the idea of the Atman, the soul-like reflection of the Godhead, present in each individual. I frequently explain the Hindu greeting, "*Namaste*," translated as "I honor (or greet) the light within you," to patients who do not have a fully differentiated sense of self, with concomitant low self-esteem. My experience has been that these people are particularly soothed and encouraged by the idea that they have an inviolable and honorable essence, separate and unique to themselves. This would reflect a type of mirroring, as seen by the Self Psychologists.

I exercise caution in recommending a meditative or contemplative practice for individuals with psychotic disorders. Concentration meditations, those that aim for a one-pointed focus of attention, generally promote physical and emotional relaxation and states of calm when practiced in moderate amounts. Transcendental Meditation, the popular and widely practiced form of concentration meditation, calls for two twenty-minute practice sessions of meditation integrated into a day otherwise oriented to mundane life activities.

My sense is that psychotic or potentially psychotic individuals may be adversely affected by both intense concentration meditation practice and intense insight practice. Intense concentration meditation practice can promote states of consciousness increasingly removed from current life experience. This would not be favorable for individuals whose primary difficulty is in relating appropriately to current life experience. Aldous Huxley borrowed from poet William Blake when he described this phenomenon as "cleansing the doors of perception." While heightened sense perception is enjoyable, indeed sought after, by individuals with well-integrated ego structures, it can be overwhelming to people with more fragile ego organization. Also, more intense concentration states sometimes include radically altered sense perception—sights, sounds, tastes, smells, and feelings can be quite different from ordinary awareness. This would clearly be stressful and confusing for someone not well oriented in time and space.

Awareness (insight) meditations are also problematic for people with fragile ego structure. These practices tend to a destabilizing of ego structure. Neurotic defenses against the emergence of unconscious material begin to drop away as people practice meditations that develop calm attention. It is quite common for meditators to discover patterns of behavior that previously were unconscious. Sometimes people discover, in the form of surprising memories and affect, early life traumata they have kept hidden from themselves for many years. For people with well-integrated ego structure, these memories are painful but useful ways to continue psychological and emotional healing. They often require the addition of psychotherapy as an adjunct to spiritual practice, in those instances when an individual is not already in therapy. For those individuals who are struggling in their lives to work with the thoughts and feelings already conscious to them, as is the case with psychotic individuals, meditation practice that is destabilizing would be an unwise course of action. Unconscious thoughts and feelings would surely be well beyond the range of material with which they could comfortably cope.

Some years ago I consulted briefly with the family of a man in his early twenties who had become very disorganized in his thinking and behavior following intense concentration meditation practice. It is important to point out that prior to his meditation experience he had been marginally functional, barely able to get through school (although his intelligence was above normal), unable to hold a job for any period of time, and unable to make any kind of meaningful or gratifying social relationships. He began practicing Transcendental Meditation and combined three- and four-hour practice sessions with long periods of fasting. It was at this point that he became more withdrawn, and subsequently his behavior became much more strange and alarming to his family.

In viewing the situation, my sense was that this young man basically had a psychotic illness and had been able, until the onset of the intense meditation practice, to lead a semblance of a "normal life" because of the structure and support afforded him within his family. They had helped him through school, supported and encouraged him in seeking new jobs, and continued to provide a home for him because he was unable to be independent. I felt their external, reality-based support was what had held his fragile psyche together. His intense meditation practice, withdrawing him from an external reality focus, coupled with fasting (which heightens the effect of meditation), seemed to have put too much strain on his poorly developed ego structure. My suggestion to this man and to his family was that he stop meditation until his life restabilized. I also recommended that he stop fasting, eat regularly, and begin an exercise program. I encouraged him to look for a meaningful job and to seek out some fellowship group, perhaps a church group, that he could join. By following these suggestions, and with the continued support of his family, he was able to recover his earlier level of functioning.

The optimal transpersonal addition to the treatment of the psychotic individual would be, I believe, a practice with some structure, a practice with relevance to daily life activity, and a practice that enhances self-esteem. The following case description shows how *A Course in Miracles* serves as just such a treatment modality. At its highest level of use, *A Course in Miracles* is intended to be a tool for spiritual transcendence. However, as is shown, it can also be used to provide structure in an otherwise structureless life. Its emphasis on forgiveness is a very important tool for people whose interpersonal relationships are impaired. Its emphasis on the sanctity of each soul is important to people without a clear sense of self or self-esteem.

Case Study: George

George is a seventy-five-year-old retired electrician whom I have been treating for thirty-five years. His presenting problems were those of rage, delusions of persecution and grandeur, schizoid isolation, and chronic depression. George's mother and several of his siblings were psychotic, diagnosed as paranoid schizophrenics. All of George's family members were described by him as having been very cold, unempathic, and subject to rages. George felt good about the work he was doing as an electrician because it permitted him to be in contact with the world doing something he considered useful. However, he had never allowed close personal contact with any individual other than myself. He had never been married. Before I began treating him, George was hospitalized on several occasions when his symptoms had been severe enough to render him nonfunctional. The episodes of hospitalization had been preceded by periods of chaotic, enraged disorganization—during which time George had become overwhelmed and confused.

George illustrates all the classic ego defects represented in paranoid schizophrenia. In terms of psychological lesions, George's major pathology may be understood as an undifferentiated ego boundary of a primitive nature. This undifferentiated boundary state causes disorganization of his thinking and functioning. He is unable to separate his internal aggressive and fearful thoughts from external events. He projects his rage onto his environment and then reacts to his environment as if it were truly threatening. The primary treatment goal has always been to keep his thinking as unconfused as possible, and this has consistently required drug therapy. Another aspect of my treatment goals was the lessening of his anger and fearfulness to provide for the possibility of more gratifying interpersonal relationships. I based this aspect of his treatment on my assumption that if his rage were diminished it would become less threatening to his already fragile ego structure. He would then not need to use projections so much as a compensatory defense and thus would, I hoped, be able to function more skillfully with others.

After beginning treatment with me, George was able to continue working more or less steadily until his recent retirement. A mainstay of his treatment was the use of a phenothiazine tranquilizer (Mellaril). The importance of that as the underpinning of his supportive psychotherapy was seen in the fact that on one occasion when (unbeknownst to me) he stopped taking his medication, he decompensated, became totally disoriented, and had to be hospitalized.

In the supportive psychotherapy aspect of George's treatment, I saw myself functioning as an auxiliary ego, helping him clarify areas of confused thinking and helping with general problem-solving. The frequency of our visits varied. During periods in which he experienced considerable discomfort, I saw him once or twice a week to ensure his continued functioning. In periods of relatively stable functioning, I saw him once a month, mainly to monitor his medication.

George's work seemed to have a stabilizing effect on him. When he was working, he required fifty mg. per day of Mellaril to keep him functioning. Between jobs, or on vacation, he would require seventy-five mg. per day to keep his psychotic processes from overwhelming him. With this in mind, I had some concern as he planned his retirement. I wondered whether his condition would worsen without the daily structure of a job to support him. I was also concerned because his job was the main area from which he derived any sense of personal worth or self-esteem, the only way in which he felt he contributed to the world or society.

I had previously found, in working with other patients with severe psychopathology, that recommending certain transpersonal reading materials to them had often had a salutary effect. I am convinced that they correctly perceived that these transpersonal issues were very important to me, and my wanting to include them in these areas of study and practice enhanced their sense of personal worthiness. The mirroring and idealizing effects spoken of by the Self Psychologists are readily visible here.

I suggested to George that he read *A Course in Miracles*. I thought it might add some structure to his schedule, as the

Course requires daily reading periods as well as practice exercises throughout the day. I specifically suggested *A Course in Miracles* because of George's Christian background and because it stresses forgiveness and the overcoming of anger, particular areas of concern for him. A further reason for recommending *A Course in Miracles* was that it can be read and practiced on one's own. Though there are *A Course in Miracles* study groups that meet together to work with the material, participation in these groups is not mandatory for practice. Given George's schizoid and paranoid nature, it would not have been possible to suggest that he involve himself in a group spiritual practice.

At the time of this writing, George has been using *A Course in Miracles* for about five years. He spends from one to three hours a day reading the *Course* and doing the exercises. He and I concur that there has been a marked decrease in his feelings of rage during this period, and I conclude that the emphasis the *Course* places on forgiveness has been effective in modulating George's aggressive drives.

I believe it's important to recognize that while practicing *A Course in Miracles* has attenuated George's aggressive drives, it has not changed his basic ego boundary defect. He continues to have bizarre thoughts, but he has restructured them so that they are less disturbing. For example, in former years he had told me that the reason his neighbor's dog came to his house and defecated on his steps was that his neighbor was angry at him. Now he feels himself responsible because he has not sent his neighbor enough loving thoughts. Clearly he is still psychotic in the sense of his overevaluating the power of his thoughts. However, although he continues to project his aggressive thoughts onto others, he has modified his formerly angry projection to a formulation that emphasizes his own lovingness.

George recently recounted a poignant story of feeling kindly toward others for the first time in his memory. He had been reading *A Course in Miracles* just prior to going to the supermarket. In the store, as he walked up and down the aisles, he realized with pleasure that he was thinking kindly thoughts. However, he also noted that by the time he got to the checkout stand this had passed, and he seemed to have closed down again, reverting to his former angry, frightened, paranoid self. What's significant here is that George had noted the change in himself and felt sad. The misanthropic world view with which he had formerly totally identified was no longer acceptable to him.

Until recently, he had estranged himself entirely from his family because of the anger he felt toward them for the poor care he felt he had received while growing up. He had shunned every possibility of interaction with them, including throwing away, unopened, any Christmas presents he received from them. Since reading about forgiveness and practicing the exercises in forgiveness which *A Course in Miracles* presents, George has begun to bring thoughts of forgiveness to work with his angry feelings about his family. He has even made a few successful attempts to contact some family members in an effort to begin to build new relationships with them. He realizes he still has great difficulties in maintaining kindly feelings toward them and others, but he notices with pleasure a positive shift in his ability to do so.

In treating George, my overall objective has always been to attenuate his feelings of anger and rage so they do not overwhelm what I see as a basic structural flaw in his ego development. My assumption is that his condition is probably a result of a genetic (biological) predisposition to the formation of this type of ego defect, coupled with the trauma of emotional non-nurturance and identification with a severely dysfunctional family. I never imagined that I could cure this basic structural defect. What I hoped was that, if his aggressive drives could be attenuated, his fragile ego would remain intact enough to permit his minimal functioning. The phenothiazine therapy and the supportive therapy were both successful (and crucial) in this regard, and *A Course in Miracles* was a valuable additional therapeutic ingredient. I believe that it bolstered George's self-esteem through its emphasis on the inherent positive specialness (God-connectedness) of each person.

I believe that therapists, in general, regard therapy with psychotic individuals as being successful when patients continue to function reasonably well on a day-to-day basis with minimal regressions. This is at the opposite end of the spectrum of growth from those individuals whom we see as having a highly consolidated, well-functioning ego—the kind of people for whom spiritual practice and ego transcendence seem most appropriate. There is obviously a crucial difference between George and those individuals who, having successfully mastered the normal levels of psychosexual development, are able to go on to begin to experience feelings of unity consciousness and undifferentiated ego boundaries. Whereas a lessening of attachment to one's personal ego may be viewed as a central goal in spiritual practice, in George's situation it was precisely the opposite—the establishment of a separate, differentiated self—that was the desired treatment goal.

For George, *A Course in Miracles*, a system designed for ego transcendence, functioned in the service of ego-building. Beginning from a schizoid, paranoid stance, he evolved toward a slightly more outer-directed, caring, or loving orientation. Even if the degree to which George's orientation away from himself is minimal, at least he has moved in what I consider to be a healthy direction.

The introduction of the practice of *A Course in Miracles* into George's life was also effective because it functioned as a positive time filler for him during his retirement. It is important to remember that George has had difficulties in the past dealing with blocks of unstructured time. *A Course in Miracles* also presents a theoretical way of understanding the world. For a man like George, who describes himself as "a man who wasn't present when the rules for understanding the world were given out," this theoretical construction is very gratifying.

During the years when I was using traditional supportive psychotherapy and medication with George, I had felt that the therapy was largely maintenance level. It was not until I began to talk about transpersonal issues with him and he began to practice *A Course in Miracles* that significant changes began to occur. *A Course in Miracles* continues to reinforce his beginning attempts to forgive his family and neighbors (and people in general) so that he can interact with them in a positive way.

Chapter 4

The Transpersonal Treatment of the
Borderline Psychotic Patient

THE BORDERLINE PSYCHOTIC PATIENT differs from the frankly psychotic patient in particular, crucial aspects. Certain characteristics that are often present in psychotic individuals, such as bizarre or irrational thoughts, hallucinations, and/or inappropriate behavior or affect, are generally absent in the borderline patient. Although there are certain ego defects present at this level of psychological organization, there may be many areas of considerable ego strength.

My working hypothesis in treating individuals with borderline pathology is that these disorders stem from a failure in ego development that occurs during the first two years of life. I believe, as I do in the case of the psychoses, that there may be a genetic predisposition to this failure of ego development. A hallmark of the borderline condition is the inability to appropriately process aggressive impulses. Adolescents who are diagnosed as being borderline psychotic often have a history of hyperactivity and hyperaggression in childhood.

The inability of the borderline patient to handle rage might be seen as a combination of genetic predispositions (often innate hyperaggression) and the failure of the proper empathic response on the part of the parental environment. The etiology seems not as significant as the consequences of this ego defect. When the ego, for whatever reason, is unable to handle aggressive feelings that are felt to be overwhelming, it resorts to "splitting the object," putting people into categories of being either all good or all bad, in order to avoid ego disintegration. In other words, in normal development, a child becomes able to tolerate the notion that he or she can, at different times, both love and hate the same individual and that neither impulse will be overwhelming. In the borderline child or adolescent, this is not possible.

Adult borderline patients show the same inability as children to integrate both loving and aggressive feelings toward the same person. They also tend to see people as "all good" or "all bad." This inevitably leads to difficulties in relationships since, in all relationships in which loving feelings originally predominated, there are inevitably periods of frustration that require the successful and appropriate expression of anger. In therapy, this sometimes is worked through when the patient, who formerly experienced the therapist as "all good" and caring, feels frustrated and angered by the therapist and needs to integrate these two feelings.

In addition to relationship problems, the borderline patient often has low self-esteem. Perhaps this is a result of the inadequate early childhood empathic nurturance experience (whatever its etiology), where the low self-esteem reflects the fact that the sense of self is poorly developed. In addition, because adults with this type of pathology have generally had difficulty in school and in relationship experiences, they have not had the chance to build self-esteem as a result of personal successes. The failure in adulthood of adequate mirroring and idealizing relationships probably compounds a preexisting failure in these areas in childhood.

The classical technique for working with borderline patients would be the building of ego strengths through identification with an empathic therapist and the repair of the "splitting of objects" through recognition of its occurrence in the transference. The Self Psychologists call this "the process of transmuting internalization," by which new and healthier psychic structures are acquired. In some cases, phenothiazines or Selective Serotonin Reuptake Inhibitors (SSRIs), e.g., Prozac, may be used to attenuate the aggressive impulses if they are too anxiety-provoking, in order to make supportive and interpretive therapy possible.

In the following four case presentations, transpersonal techniques were used in addition to traditional therapy to facilitate the treatment. I have seen how certain techniques, borrowed from traditional spiritual practices, can be used specifically to attenuate anger, to enhance a sense of personal self-worth, and to increase the capacity for self-observation, a particular ego strength often lacking in the borderline patient.

———————————— *Case Study: Ben* ————————————

The following case material is particularly instructive since Ben, prior to the critical period in which I saw him, had appeared reasonably well integrated. At the time that I met him, Ben was thirty-two years old, married, and had one child. He had been working for some time as a paramedic. Responding to a medical emergency, he had apparently not done a particular procedure correctly, and the patient had suffered some permanent damage. Ben was strongly criticized by his co-workers, and he had felt both remorse and strong humiliation. After this incident, which he felt was very traumatic, he had become increasingly psychologically disorganized. He left that job, started work as a heavy equipment operator, but eventually was unable to work at all because his newly developed paranoid system, involving feelings of persecution, was making it impossible for him to relate to others.

Although I took a careful developmental history, I could not see any clear source for this fairly severe psychopathological condition. There had been no periods of severe emotional difficulty during Ben's childhood or adolescence. Furthermore, prior to his current symptoms, Ben's marriage had appeared to be reasonably gratifying and stable. Because of the level and type of disorganization manifested in a previously well-functioning individual, I felt that the most adequate diagnosis for Ben would be that of the borderline psychotic personality. The traditional treatment for him would have included phenothiazine along with some type of supportive psychotherapy. After we began therapy, Ben wanted to return to work, but, because his work was operating heavy machinery, a job that required precision and dexterity, he was reluctant to take tranquilizers. The use of any phenothiazine often produces the side effect of sleepiness or diminution of reflexes, and I therefore supported Ben's decision in this regard.

I saw Ben weekly for supportive psychotherapy. To counteract his preoccupation with paranoid, fear-producing thoughts, I suggested that he study *A Course in Miracles*. Ben found the practice of the daily meditations helpful in a non-traditional way. Normally, these meditations are reflections on metaphysical truths upon which one is meant to ruminate. Ben would recite the daily meditations over and over to himself in the style with which one might use a mantra. As it turned out, rather than using the meditations as a contemplative exercise, Ben used them as a concentration meditation. To the degree that Ben was able to keep his mind occupied with the meditation, his delusional thoughts were prevented from overwhelming him.

There were, therefore, three ways in which Ben's use of the daily reflections in *A Course in Miracles* were helpful to him. His recitations, in mantra style, provided the calming effect on both mind and body common to concentration meditations. Secondly, Ben's use of the recitations in mantra style excluded his disturbing thoughts. The third benefit Ben derived from his practice related to the circumstance of his being a practicing Catholic. Ben retained good feelings about his church affiliation, and so the Christian terminology of *A Course in Miracles* was comforting to him.

Another somewhat radical treatment intervention on my part was to advise Ben to stop listening to the news on radio or TV and to stop reading newspapers. He had used the generally negative and often violent information he got from these sources to reinforce and justify his paranoid world view. Ben was willing to follow my advice. As his exposure to these negative stimuli was reduced and his positive thoughts generated by his *Course in Miracles* meditations increased, his paranoia and delusions faded and then entirely disappeared.

I believe that doing *A Course in Miracles* meditations replaced the use of phenothiazines in subduing Ben's disturbed thoughts. His meditations, which he carried on throughout much of the day, seemed to provide periods of tranquillity in which his ego was able to reintegrate. In our therapy sessions together, I focused on supporting his positive efforts to reconstruct his daily life. We talked about his relationships with his wife and his children. I supported his efforts to get a new job and encouraged him to try to build friendships with co-workers. I believe this somewhat mundane, seemingly trivial, advice was a valuable therapeutic intervention since it conveyed to him the idea that I thought he was a valuable enough person to have as a friend. I think his sense of self-worth was further heightened by the fact that when I explained *A Course in Miracles* practice to him I told him that I did this practice as well. Because the precipitating event leading to the onset of his symptoms (his mistake as a paramedic) was the strong trauma to his already shaky sense of self-worth, his seeing that I related to him as a person worthy of respect was probably the most valuable part of our psychotherapeutic interchange. Also, since *A Course in Miracles* emphasizes forgiveness, I believe that practicing the meditations in the *Course* strengthened Ben's ability to forgive himself for his mistake.

From a Self Psychology point of view, there were positive mirroring and idealizing experiences for Ben, both from me and from the author of *A Course in Miracles*. Ben made a remarkably swift complete recovery from symptoms. He was able to return to work on a full-time basis, and his paranoid ideation disappeared, as did his preoccupation with his feelings of guilt. He continued to do his mantra meditation using *A Course in Miracles*. Ben's rapid recovery was a result, I believe, of 1) supportive psychotherapy, in which we emphasized talking about his experience and his feelings in a way that allowed him to get some balanced distance from them, and 2) his mantra practice. Furthermore I believe that a major component of his successful recovery was his positive identification with me based on his sense of my acceptance of him. I think this was facilitated both by the soothing effect of his mantra practice and by the avoidance of agitating negative stimuli.

A significant aspect of the next case study is the apparent presence of psychic healing powers in this patient, which initially led me to overestimate his level of psychological development. Whereas traditional therapy has disregarded psychic phenomena or has regarded their presence as pathologic, I believe transpersonal therapists, in their enthusiastic respect for such phenomena, often overvalue their presence. We may erroneously take them to be reflections of advanced spiritual and psychological growth, when they actually may reflect a pre-neurotic psychological organization.

Case Study: Henry

Henry is a forty-one-year-old administrator in a county social service agency. He sought treatment for his depression at the time of the breakup of his second marriage. Henry had a history of severe depressions alternating with rage, periodic overeating, alcoholism, hypochondria, and severe authority figure problems. His father, a career diplomat, had been exceedingly harsh in his criticism of him. Henry had perceived his mother as being totally unsupportive, unempathic, and rejecting. Henry had married twice, and both marriages had failed, primarily because of the tension generated by his symptoms, especially his rage.

When I first interviewed Henry, I mistakenly judged his level of psychological development to be higher than it was. In retrospect, this was probably because, as a social worker, he was relatively fluent in psychological language. Also, I was probably impressed by his lifelong interest in transpersonal psychology, the paranormal, and especially in psychic phenomena and healing. Ten years before I met him he had begun to attend healing groups and to visit a psychic to seek psychological guidance. He claimed, and I felt it might be true, that he sometimes intuitively knew a great deal about other people and that he was sometimes helpful as a healer.

Prior to seeing me, Henry had been in psychotherapy on two occasions, both times briefly and in periods of particular stress. On various occasions, he had been given tranquilizers and antidepressants for symptomatic relief. Although Henry had a fairly high intellectual capacity, having graduated from a prestigious university, and held an administrative position in his agency, the severity of his symptoms prompted me to have psychological testing done. My own sense was that he had been traumatized during the first few years of life by a massive failure in empathic relationships with his inadequate mother and wrathful father. Positive mirroring and idealizing experiences were almost absent. I felt that the classical diagnosis would be that of borderline personality with narcissistic features. This diagnosis was corroborated by the psychologist who did the testing.

My primary aim in Henry's treatment was to be supportive of him during his divorce crisis. Because his intellectual strengths were good and he was relatively conversant about psychology and psychodynamics, he could use intellectual defenses skillfully. He was able to talk about his hypercritical parents in a way that maintained distance from his affect. Given the basically fragile nature of his ego structure and the difficulties Henry had in maintaining an observant ego while under stress, I hesitated to push for a more deeply interpretive meaning to his symptoms. He soon experienced considerable symptom relief, and he was able to function fairly well on a day-to-day basis.

In order to strengthen his observing ego capacities, I suggested that Henry practice Vipassana meditation. He went to some introductory classes and attended several weekend and week-long retreats in the practice of this method. Henry felt that these experiences were helpful to him, and I agreed. His symptoms lessened.

The initial stages of practice of Vipassana meditation essentially consist of a concentration meditation to settle and focus the awareness; this generally has a calming effect for individuals at all stages of ego development. In addition, I've noticed that learning to examine the arising and passing away of successive moments of experience has the effect of strengthening the sense of observing ego.

Here is an example from Henry's retreat experience. Retreatants met in small group sessions led by a teacher, in which they reported their meditation experience. Henry told me that during these small group interviews he frequently felt other meditators did not seem to be interested in what he had to say. He said he would characteristically become angry at what he interpreted as their lack of interest and would ruminate about it for several hours after the group interview. He was able to notice, however, that when he returned to his meditation bench and brought his attention to his breath, as he had been instructed to do, his anger would subside. When he had a thought that recalled the interview, his anger would arise afresh, but he was often sufficiently calm to observe that the anger would subside again if he practiced focused attention to breathing. This "new-found" discovery—that he was not a victim of his affect, but rather somewhat in control of it—allowed Henry to develop some insight about the fragility of his sense of personal worth. He told me that although he had nourished the idea of himself as a superior person endowed with particular psychic gifts, he could see he was actually quite insecure. In other circumstances, this particular insight might have been intolerable to Henry's fragile ego. Nurtured by the sense of being part of a spiritual community, and indeed relaxed by the hours he spent in silent meditation, Henry seemed to be able to metabolize these psychological awarenesses.

After the retreat, when Henry recounted his psychological insight to me, I praised his ability to maintain this insight even though it was a difficult one for him to acknowledge. I encouraged him to keep up his meditation practice, reminding him that his former feelings of being overwhelmed with affect had made it difficult for him to look deeply at his core psychological issues. I expressed my confidence that he would now be able to use psychotherapy even more effectively. I believe my expression of confidence bolstered his self-esteem. He seemed able, in subsequent months of therapy, to talk about his childhood and his disappointing two marriages with more affect. Henry's depression lifted considerably, and therapy was ended when he was offered a good job in another state six months later.

Another component to my work with Henry was his interest in and study of *A Course in Miracles*. As our relationship developed and he came to trust and admire me, he would ask me for suggestions for readings that he might do in the area of spirituality. Among the books that I suggested was *A Course in Miracles*. Interest in the *Course* varies, I have discovered, from person to person, depending on the affinity they have with the Christian basis of the *Course* or with the patriarchal tone of it. Henry liked it a lot. He was able to translate the exercises of the *Course* into the practice of forgiveness toward his parents, himself, and his former wives.

Henry's work with *A Course in Miracles* was helpful to the therapy since it began to make his angry response ego alien. Henry's habit had been to operate at a high level of rage, often accompanied by feelings of self-justification. Although his anger was clearly disabling and self-defeating, in the beginning of the therapy I thought it would be counterproductive to mobilize further anger toward me by pointing this out to him. Having the neutral intermediary of *A Course in Miracles* address the question of anger and the need for forgiveness lessened the risk of bringing on a severe negative transference reaction to me. This permitted an ongoing good working alliance between myself and Henry and ultimately led to his experiencing less anger and achieving better self-control. In the beginning of our work together, it seemed to me that reducing Henry's anger by an indirect and neutral means would be the most therapeutic course. His presenting complaint of severe depression seemed a reflection of his anger, and his anger felt, to him, too strong and potentially destructive to express. Reducing the intensity of his anger, therefore, seemed the most expeditious thing to do. With the lowering of his overall tension level, Henry was able to build new ego strengths. We continued to have a good working relationship, and he became increasingly able to confront the roots of anger in his life. Usually, Henry would be angry at me when he perceived me as acting like one of his parents. In those instances where he was misperceiving my response, these transference distortions could be pointed out and worked through. In those instances where, for whatever reason, I had truly not been empathic with him, he was able to reexperience the pain of having had nonempathic parents, come to some acceptance of it, and proceed in a more integrated, relaxed way than he had previously.

 Both transpersonal additions to Henry's therapy—Vipassana meditation and *A Course in Miracles*—functioned as necessary components of ongoing therapy. Henry relished the idea that he was "on a spiritual path." He identified with his teachers, whom he admired. He seemed to experience the receiving of spiritual teachings as being "fed by the spiritual knowledge of the ages," and this strengthened him. Both Vipassana meditation and *A Course in Miracles* were used for the lessening of anger, the practicing of forgiveness, and, perhaps even more importantly, the building of structure via the internalization of the values of the parent-teacher figure. Both practices nurtured Henry's sense of self-esteem, and he used both to build and consolidate ego strengths. This further enabled him to go on to do more intense psychotherapeutic work.

Case Study: David

David was a married forty-one-year-old typesetter at a large advertising agency who was referred for psychotherapy by a psychiatrist on the Vocational Rehabilitation Disability Board after he had become so depressed and disorganized that he was unable to work. He experienced suicidal thoughts. David felt that he was being unfairly harassed on the job. Although there was some validity to his feelings of being unfairly treated, the extent of his rage and the severity of his depression were suggestive of severe pathology. David feared that he would kill his supervisor. The referring psychiatrist diagnosed him as a borderline psychotic personality with an ego boundary defect.

I agreed with the referring psychiatrist that the degree of David's rage and his feelings of paranoia were suggestive of considerable pathology in the area of basic ego boundaries. David had been reared in the rural South by harsh parents. He reported that he had been a bed wetter until the age of twelve and had always been frightened of the dark. In high school he had felt that others were talking about him, and throughout his life his jealousy and violent temper had gotten him into many difficulties. Although capable at his job, his appearance and manner were rough and unsophisticated. He used alcohol and marijuana frequently, probably in attempts to tranquilize his rage.

Considering David's modest level of education, I was not hopeful, given the degree of pathology that seemed present as well, that I could effect any major changes in basic psychopathology. I thought supportive psychotherapy and the use of a mild tranquilizer might lessen his feelings of rage and depression, and this would then attenuate the stress being experienced by his fragile ego structure. I saw David once a week in supportive psychotherapy. In addition, I prescribed a mild tranquilizer for him. The psychotherapy was generally instructive rather than interpretive. In other words, without challenging his paranoid thought system, I helped him think through what might be more effective ways of relating to his present life situation.

When I tried to evaluate David's areas of interest, I learned that he liked to read books about how the world originated and how the universe "worked." I therefore provided David with a large bibliography of spiritual literature, which he read with enthusiasm. He was especially soothed and inspired by stories about individuals, such as saints and gurus in various traditions, who had achieved high levels of spiritual attainment

Because I had been the inspiration for David to read spiritual literature, he projected onto me the idea that I was a particularly spiritually advanced individual. He imagined that I operated on the same level of spiritual attainment as the saints and gurus he was reading about. Although I certainly did not do anything to agree with or encourage this fantasied point of view, neither did I particularly discourage it or interpret it. It seemed to me that the combination of his inflated esteem for me and his recognition of my acceptance of him increased his self-confidence. The mirroring and idealizing aspects of our relationship seemed to be a healing force in the repair of his sense of self. Another way of describing this would be to say that there was a process of repairing David's ego defect through a healthy identification with me. As his therapy progressed, he seemed to be able to show a reasonable amount of healthy assertiveness without being troubled by overwhelming rage.

I sent David to a mindfulness meditation retreat, where he received basic instructions, and he practiced diligently, appropriately incorporating the techniques into his daily activities. His mindfulness practice was so continuous through much of the day (driving, working, etc.), that it served to eliminate almost entirely his obsessional ruminations.

David's meditation practice seemed to lead to a strengthening of his faculty of observing ego. As he became able to observe the arising and passing away of different emotions, he became more able to maintain an observing distance from these emotions, rather than becoming caught up in and acting upon them. It also seemed to me that, in addition to his growing ability to observe his changing emotions, he was increasingly able to make these observations from a place of apparent equanimity. The more he was able to develop this dispassionate sense of witnessing, the stronger his impulse control became.

The style in which David practiced mindfulness was a particularly potent factor in his being able to use it to develop dispassionate observing awareness. David used the technique of naming his experiences in a way that was similar to his other obsessive preoccupations. He named every single moment of experience. Although the technique of naming, as it is taught in Vipassana meditation, is meant to serve as a tool to incline the mind primarily to the passing nature of all experience, David named so minutely and so continuously as to preclude the arising of any tangential thoughts. In this way, his naming practice served as a mantra practice, deepening his concentration by making his focus of attention steadfastly one-pointed. For example, while driving his car, he would make mental notes of "shifting, steering, braking, etc." By using all the movements of his daily, mundane experience as the focus of his attention, he was able to block out all negative and upsetting thoughts. He practiced the same one-pointed focus in his work situation. He was fascinated and gratified by the good feelings he experienced while naming and so developed the habit of naming throughout the day. He reported to me that on certain occasions when the activity itself was quite mundane, his naming process went on intensely and so continuously that he would be filled with feelings of rapture. Somewhat naively, he considered the idea of trying to convert all of his co-workers to mindfulness meditation. I suggested to him that he restrain this impulse. Because I knew his co-workers already regarded him as being somewhat odd, I wanted to spare him the possibility of feeling in any way disparaged or ridiculed by them.

David's delight in his meditation practice also produced some unusual discord with his wife. After David's first ten-day mindfulness retreat, he reported to me that he was getting up very early each morning to meditate. His wife, he said, expressed anger that he seemed to care more about meditation than he did about staying in bed with her. This dilemma was easily solved. I reminded him that the Buddha taught that mindfulness could happen in all positions, including lying down. Thereafter, when David awakened early, he lay in bed and named body sensations to himself as a way of meditating without leaving his wife.

I also taught David a forgiveness meditation. Forgiveness meditations exist in all the spiritual disciplines I know. I believe this is because forgiveness is the necessary prerequisite to being able to express oneself lovingly and compassionately. David had been particularly impressed by his Buddhist teachers in his mindfulness course, so I taught him a meditation from the Buddhist tradition.

In Buddhist practice, forgiveness meditation precedes *metta* (lovingkindness) meditations, the directing of good wishes toward others. In the forgiveness preamble to *metta*, meditators recognize the possibility that they might have inadvertently hurt others, and they hope to be forgiven for this unskillful behavior. Likewise, the meditators recognize that others, equally unskillful, have offended them, and they cultivate forgiveness of them. The repetition of this intention seemed to provide a very effective tool for David to reduce his feelings of rage and anger. The lessening of rage toward oneself as well as toward others always brings with it an increase in the sense of self-esteem.

It is important to emphasize that at no time did I use interpretive techniques with David, linking his rage with his pathologic family background. I had the concern that interpretive techniques might prove overwhelming to his already fragile ego structure. He improved dramatically and was able to go back to work in his original job. Treatment was concluded following fourteen months of once-a-week psychotherapy sessions.

I was fortunate to be able to obtain a sixteen-year follow up on David: his wife told me that their marriage continued to go well. David told me that he did one or two hours of (walking) mindfulness meditation every day and also continued to incorporate meditation into his daily work. He reported that he feels cheerful "most of the time" and is so effective on the job that he was recently rated best employee of the year. Although his manner is still unsophisticated and his reading limited to a few favorite texts, he seemed truly comfortable with the idea that difficulties are a part of life and are bearable. He explained his acceptance of suffering as being a result of knowing that "everything is impermanent and changing." Perhaps, because of David's limited education and rather severe psychopathology, I erred in underestimating the degree to which meditation practice could lead to genuine spiritual insight.

Case Study: Doris

Doris was a thirty-five-year-old married woman with two children, who worked as a salesperson. She came into therapy because of an ongoing depression, difficulties in communicating with her husband, a vague sense of distress about how her life was going, and an uneasiness about rearing her two teenage daughters. She was a college graduate with a degree in journalism. Although she had never sought psychotherapy for her depression, she had frequently consulted with psychics to consider what she should do in the future. She periodically practiced a meditation that she felt evoked protective powers for herself and her family.

My work with Doris demonstrates how it is possible for an individual to have a "transpersonal-looking" belief system, and yet be unable to benefit from it. In fact, Doris used a somewhat skewed interpretation of the spiritual value of forgiveness as a defense against dealing with the pre-neurotic problem of appropriate recognition and expression of anger.

When I began treating Doris, I used a traditional, psychoanalytically oriented, interpretive approach. It initially seemed to me that her major difficulty was that of poor communication with her husband, especially in the area of her aggressive feelings. She was unable to express even the mildest irritation with her husband or with her daughters. Her overall level of ego functioning seemed to me at the time to be relatively strong. She was, and continues to be, a devoted mother who is very conscientious about her children's welfare.

It was my hope that traditional psychotherapy would lessen her defenses against the awareness of strong affect, primarily rage. I also felt some unconscious libidinal issues might emerge as well, and these might be what lay behind her uneasiness in relating to her teenage daughters. However, as therapy proceeded there was no emergence or resolution of oedipal issues. Instead, what became unmasked was a much deeper psychopathology which apparently began manifesting in previous periods of disorganization, suicide attempts, and dissociative episodes. In these episodes, Doris had experienced loss of contact with reality in varying degrees, reflecting attempts by her psyche to block the awareness of anger from her consciousness. She "confessed" that these symptoms had been present since her adolescence, but that she had been "too embarrassed" to reveal this material in our earlier interviews.

Probably as a reflection of her own pathology, Doris had been working with psychics and meditational systems from which she had synthesized a transpersonal belief system that emphasized "all is lovingness and kindness." It became clear to me that she used this belief system to avoid coming to grips with the enormous rage she felt toward her parents, children, husband, and me—all of whom she over-idealized. Later on in her treatment, as she trusted me more, she was better able to describe the severity of the cold, non-caring home from which she had come. Her parents live nearby and continue to rebuff her attempts to establish a warm relationship with them.

Even when Doris finally began to be aware of her rage and disappointment with her parents, she was still not able to express her feelings. My guess would be that the etiology of her psychological condition derives from the first year or two of her life, when she had no choice but to split off the positive feelings she had for her parents from her negative feelings toward them in order to "protect" them from her rage.

Feeling that no progress was forthcoming from my psychotherapeutic attempts, I referred Doris to a hypnotherapist in an attempt to retrieve some of the rage issues that were lost because of her dissociative episodes. I felt Doris would be amenable to going because of her previous interest in psychics and psychic phenomena. Doris agreed to hypnotherapy and appeared to be a willing and responsive participant in the therapy sessions. However, although the tapes of these therapy sessions seemed to disclose experiences and emotions from her past, in the periods after the hypnosis she was not willing to listen to the material and considered it to be valueless. Her need to avoid being aware of her rage was so great that she would dissociate even while listening to tapes of her own hypnotherapy sessions.

I had hoped the hypnotherapy would at least be relaxing and might give Doris some tools for beginning to look at, and work with, her anger. I was not concerned about whether the "past-life" experiences were "actual" past-life experiences, archetypal experiences, or related to current dream experiences. I hoped she would be able to use the material either as an explanation of her current problems or a metaphor for her current situation—anything that would make her more comfortable and thus better prepared to work with her rage. Contrary to what I hoped, with the passage of time Doris's condition worsened. Her severe dissociative episodes and suicidal behavior multiplied, and she became increasingly impaired. Her high level of anxiety precluded her going to work or functioning adequately at home. As her depression increased and I could see more instances of "splitting" present in her psychological functioning, I realized the more appropriate initial diagnosis would have been borderline psychotic with ego defects. At this point, I prescribed phenothiazine tranquilizers for Doris, and these seemed somewhat helpful. The tranquilizers served to lessen the aggressive drives, so that her already weakened ego structure did not feel so overwhelmed. In her therapy sessions, I tried to be as supportive as I could of her attempts to deal with her now-stressful family situation, and I made no attempts at interpretive psychotherapy.

At one juncture, when Doris seemed particularly fragile, it was necessary to hospitalize her for several weeks. In the hospital setting, removed from the stress   she feels dealing with her husband and daughters, she did not experience any of her dissociative episodes. This was a very important observation, since it confirmed the hypothesis that her dissociative episodes occur entirely as a defense against the awareness and expression of anger.

I believe Doris had embraced a transpersonal belief system and practiced a meditative technique from that system particularly because they both reinforced her denial of the presence of her angry feelings. It is true that many transpersonal techniques derive from spiritual traditions that stress kindness and emphasize the use of forgiveness in overcoming anger. However, from the point of view of psychological development, the ability to be aware of the presence of angry or aggressive feelings is crucial. A psychologically mature individual, when aware of angry or aggressive feelings, has at least two options for dealing with these feelings. The first is to find a skillful way of communicating angry feelings so that whatever gave rise to them can be considered thoughtfully by all persons involved, in order that a more successful relationship can be worked out. The second option may be utilized in place of, or as a preparation for, communicating those feelings. This option is the practice of a forgiveness technique, which might help attenuate the feelings of anger. Both the skillful expression and the transmutation of feelings of anger are obviously very different from either repressing them or denying they exist.

With continued supportive care and continued use of mild tranquilizers, Doris was able to leave the hospital, return home, and, in time, go back to her job. Both daughters have, at this point, become more independent and their school situation has stabilized, so they represent less stress for her. Her husband, through participation in family group therapy sessions during Doris's hospitalization, has become more supportive of her.

My impression is that I probably will continue to see Doris in once-a-week supportive psychotherapy for some considerable time. My hope is that perhaps when her daughters leave home altogether and there is less stress in the household, she will feel able to function on her own. Doris practices a wide variety of concentration meditation techniques, either for "protection" or for relaxation, and since her practice of these techniques is neither frequent nor intense, I encourage her to continue with it.

In reviewing these four cases of individuals with borderline psychotic conditions, certain general conclusions seem appropriate. All of these individuals seemed characterized by generally fragile ego structure, and all of the therapeutic attempts were intended to build and consolidate ego development. Interpretive therapy was avoided except in those cases where some intellectual awareness about the etiology of the condition might serve as an intellectual defense, itself an ego strength. Meditations and other transpersonal techniques were prescribed for their ego-building, rather than ego-transcending, qualities. Here too, the healing aspects of the mirroring, idealizing, and twinship relationships could be seen. Because all of the borderline conditions were characterized by problems of excessive rage and/or the expression of rage, transpersonal tools that emphasize forgiveness were often prescribed.

I cannot overemphasize how particularly instructive the cases of Henry and Doris were to me. In both cases, my initial overestimation of their level of ego development was probably a result of my being misled by their interest in psychic phenomena. My own interest in transpersonal development and psychic phenomena prejudiced me in the direction of seeing these as manifestations of fairly advanced ego development. In the cases of Henry and Doris, these "transpersonal" interests and abilities were, in one case, unrelated to psychological development and, in the other, used as a defense against psychological insight. I want to emphasize that it is important to realize there is not necessarily *any* correlation between psychic powers, levels of maturity, and spiritual attainment.

Chapter 5

The Transpersonal Treatment
of Mood Disorders

WRITING THIS CHAPTER ON MOOD DISORDERS presented certain unique problems. The two cases described are those of manic-depressive disorders. In both, the patients had been long-term meditators and spiritual seekers. Because an acute manic episode frequently is accompanied by a grandiosity and even by what appear to be genuine spiritual experiences—along with a breakdown of normal ego functioning in varying degrees—I found myself in the position of suggesting a cessation of all meditation and spiritual activity. What was emphasized, rather, was the need to focus on reintegrating day-to-day functioning in the world, along with protecting the patients and their families from the destructive behavior that so often accompanies manic-depressive disorders. Any "spiritual" insights are rarely able to be held by the weakened or disintegrating ego structure.

Patients with severe depressions present special puzzles in relationship to spiritual practices. It is fairly well accepted by the field of psychiatry (including Freudian analysts) that severe depressions have a significant primary biologic etiology.

My experience with severely depressed patients is that they do not have the energy required nor the willpower to do any spiritual exercises or practices. Fortunately, today there are many new pharmacologic agents like Prozac (and other related drugs) which can successfully reverse the symptoms of severe depression—often very dramatically and relatively rapidly.

Once the patient is restored to some level of psychological and physical energy, many of the aforementioned spiritual exercises and practices can be of further help. Depending on what the remaining (and less severe) depression is focused on, such things as meditation, forgiveness practices, and inspirational spiritual readings can be of great help in conjunction with traditional psychotherapy.

The first patient presented in this section had what he called "spiritual experiences" during a manic illness that followed a classic bipolar picture. It was important for the clinician to make a differential diagnosis here between an emerging spiritual consciousness and/or an inappropriate and out-of-balance way of thinking that reflects an underlying psychopathology.

At the present time, the evidence is quite compelling that predisposition to bipolar (manic-depressive) illness has a very strong genetic basis. When these patients are in remission, they appear to be normal, with the usual sets of characterological styles and patterns found in the general population. Ongoing daily medication of Lithium or Depakote is usually prescribed to prevent recurrences of the illness once the manic-depressive pattern is established. If there are psychotic features present during the episode, an anti-psychotic medication such as Mellaril or Haldol might be added during the acute phase.

In the following case presentation, nothing "transpersonal" was added other than an understanding and empathy for the spiritual yearning that the patient had. This greatly helped keep intact the working alliance we had before, during, and after the manic episodes. This empathic alliance was especially important because I frequently had to threaten the patient with involuntary hospitalization (to protect him and his family from his destructive actions).

───────────────── *Case Study: Harold* ─────────────────

Harold was a fifty-five-year-old art dealer whom I saw off and on over a ten-year period whenever he would have manifestations of his bipolar illness (episodes of mania or depression).

He experienced his first manic episode as a college student during his early twenties. He had six blood relatives diagnosed with this illness, including his father and grandfather.

He had a long-term, reasonably stable and gratifying marriage and spent much of his non-working time helping rear his three daughters and pursuing the "spiritual life." The latter included many meditation retreats, which he handled quite well. During one of the manic episodes earlier in his life, a vision of Jesus appeared to him and reassured him. Jesus told him that life was all about loving one another. He further reassured the patient that our soul was immortal and working its way back to the consciousness of being unified with God, and that really we are all one with God. In other visions, the patient was told that he would meet the souls of his deceased loved ones after his own death. For obvious reasons this, too, was reassuring. Along with this there were many psychotic omnipotent fantasies. Harold was on long-term Lithium medication to prevent recurrence of his manic episodes. Wanting to reexperience the profound joy of having Jesus appear to him, he would "forget" to take his Lithium medication to try to bring back what he called his "most profound religious experience."

In the early phases of an oncoming manic episode, Harold would often try to stay up all night in order to meditate. Clinicians familiar with this illness know that sleep deprivation, in susceptible individuals, can often bring on a manic episode. Here again, it was important to maneuver between honoring his spiritual aspirations and accomplishments (which were many) and his need to sleep, in order to slow down or abort the manic episode.

Usually during these times, his family would call me, rarely the patient himself. Treatment for the full-blown manic episodes frequently required hospitalization with antipsychotic medications along with Lithium or Depakote.

I was faced with an interesting dilemma. A non-transpersonal therapist would have used hospitalization, and anti-psychotic medications (if necessary) plus Lithium or Depakote would have had an excellent effect on the illness.

But Harold had been a serious spiritual seeker his entire life. Should one denigrate his spiritual vision by saying that his religious experiences are only part of his psychotic process? Do we really know how or why a spiritual experience occurs? Individuals have had profound religious or spiritual experiences with LSD or other mind-altering chemicals. Does the chemical (LSD, etc., or natural brain chemicals that operate to cause or precipitate a manic episode) cause the spiritual vision or just alter our brain apparatus to open a "window" to another level of consciousness or dimension of reality?

My approach to Harold during these episodes, along with medications, was to accept and honor any of his religious experiences as being valid (for him) and even perhaps desirable for many of us. However, I did keep the psychotherapy focus on how unbalanced he was during his spiritual experiences. I would often use the analogy that his content could be valid, but his container was having trouble integrating his visions with his everyday life. Here, for example, his megalomania would take the form of spending large sums of money on art objects, which would bankrupt the family if not stopped.

Although some of the manic episodes had spiritual visions and themes to them, many were non-spiritual in content. This was especially so when Harold would use alcohol during a manic episode, at which time he would become hyperaggressive, sadistic, and destructive to himself and his family. He later would tell me that during these episodes he was possessed by demonic forces and that the good forces within him were losing. He would say that he wanted these evil forces to come to the surface so that he could battle with them and defeat them. Unfortunately, when the destructive forces did emerge he never was able to "defeat" them without the help of medication.

Although manic episodes are quite dramatic and not too difficult to diagnose, it is important for the transpersonal therapist to keep track of the major problem here, which is the usual non-functionality of the patient, whether the manic period is manifesting as a spiritual or non-spiritual experience.

When an acute manic episode subsided with the help of Lithium medication, Harold would wistfully return to his regular life: meditating, praying, and studying. Although he fully realized that he had not been functioning while in a manic state, there was some regret that he couldn't stay with the "spiritual" joy he experienced.

During his periods of depression there were never any psychotic manifestations in his thinking or actions.

In the post-psychotic phases it was possible to help Harold translate the loving messages contained in Jesus's teachings to him during his vision period.

This was especially true as applied to the narcissistic and selfish aspects of his personality, e.g., he would express opinions about what his wife and family should be doing or how they should live their lives, with little regard for their needs. He wanted them to meditate and pray as he did.

Using positive messages from his vision of Jesus, we were able to focus on the fact that he needed to be more respectful of the other souls (wife and children) who were co-journeyers (on their own paths) to finding God. He was able to see that although his intent was good, he often expressed himself in unthoughtful and selfish ways. We were able to work with his sense of deprivation in early childhood, of never having been able to do things as he wanted to do them. As a child he had felt obliged to obey his parents' every whim lest they withdraw what little emotional support they did give him. He had felt that he had to live his life to glorify his parents' needs and that they (much like Harold with his *own* family) had shown little regard for his and his sibling's emotional needs.

Case Study: Ken

Ken is a fifty-year-old real estate agent who was brought to me by his fiancee because of grandiose delusional thinking. For the preceding four weeks Ken had felt that he was in contact with extraterrestrials who were guiding him in how best to heal the planet. There were further notions about the cosmology of the universe and our place in it. This current episode was to train Ken to "command a spaceship."

Significant background information included the fact that both his mother and father had been very depressed during much of Ken's early years. In addition, there was severe depression present among many close relatives. Despite his parents' being unable to nurture him, Ken matured remarkably well, became a leader in high school and college, and got married shortly after graduation. His marriage seemed to have been a good one, and he had two sons and a daughter. His outgoing personality played a role in his being successful in the real estate business. About twenty-six years earlier, he had gone through a bout of depression, which had subsided by itself after six months without treatment. Five years before, his wife had died after a long and lingering illness, during which Ken had attended her day and night with great loss of sleep. Shortly after her death, he was hospitalized with delusions of having healing powers in his hands. He was given one injection of Haldol and by the next morning appeared totally normal and was discharged from the hospital with no further problems.

For the past fifteen years Ken has considered himself a spiritual seeker and has observed a daily routine of yoga and meditation. In addition, he has spent time with many gurus, mostly those with a Hindu lineage.

The current episode seemed to have been precipitated after Ken spent some time in a meditation retreat with an Indian guru who was known for giving *Shaktipat*. This is thought to transmit a type of psychic energy that can induce in its recipient certain altered mental states, which sometimes include the automatic and uncontrolled flailing of limbs (called *Kriyas*). Unfortunately, most gurus do not take into account the mental state of the recipient of this energic transfer; sometimes, as in this situation, the results can be disastrous. Within a day, Ken's grandiose thoughts began, intermingled with bizarre yoga-like posturing which conveyed secret and special meanings.

> Although there was some thinking and replaying of hurt feelings regarding the parents' rejections early in life, most of Ken's mental content was focused on saving the planet from impending doom.

It was my knowledge and appreciation of the spiritual dimension that permitted Ken to trust me enough to take the medication (in this case, Depakote) I prescribed, even though he was resistant about losing his special "connection" to higher cosmic beings.

As in the first case, my transpersonal approach permitted me both to express appreciation about his past spiritual efforts and to insist that for the time being all efforts to do yoga and meditate be stopped. I used the analogy of the medication's strengthening his (mental) container so that his aspirations to help and heal the planet could be better focused.

Within a few days of starting the medication, his non-sleeping pattern diminished and became normal, and shortly thereafter he seemed to be totally normal, i.e., back to the pre-illness mode of thinking. The next few weeks were spent helping Ken integrate what had happened. Now, having had two episodes of mania, it will be wise for him to remain on Depakote and not allow any teacher to give him *Shaktipat*.

Chapter 6

The Transpersonal Treatment of
Pre-Neurotic Character Disorders

THE PREDOMINANT FEATURE that distinguishes the pre-neurotic character illnesses from borderline psychotic conditions is the absence of ego defects. Individuals at this level of psychodynamic integration do not show any real problems of ego boundary distortions. There is no evidence of bizarre or irrational thought processes such as those that characterize the psychotic or borderline psychotic conditions. My hypothesis is that individuals with character illness have consolidated most of the ego development that appropriately occurs in the first few years of life. Nevertheless, they seem to exhibit emotional fixations which are the sequelae of a variety of possible traumata that may have occurred during these early years. A lack of nurturance may lead to excessive dependency needs. Overindulgence may lead to problems in the areas of self-control and the appropriate expression of aggression. It seems possible for either over- or underindulgence to lead to a sense of narcissistic "entitlement," the sense that one may do as one pleases without respect for the needs of others. People with character pathology are often described as "selfish."

In addition, a high level of aggression seems characteristic of this level of pathology. Often this can be directly related to an extremely authoritarian parenting figure during the first three years of life, when basic socialization takes place. Overly rigid, non-empathic, demanding parents leave little room for the healthy development of ego autonomy and self-esteem. Also, as children with these character problems grow up, their own difficulties in relating empathically with others usually lead to unsatisfactory life experiences, which then reinforce their already low self-esteem.

The classical treatment of individuals with character problems includes some interpretive therapy. An individual's character pathology or style will tend to be reactivated in the treatment situation just as it manifests in life situations. The maladaptive ways that a patient behaves in therapy, such as coming late for appointments, not paying the bill, finding fault with the therapist, the office, and the time of the appointment, are usually reflections of the maladaptive ways in which that person behaves in life. It is often possible to point out where such patients have a sense of "entitlement," the sense that the world ought to work in a certain way to meet their needs. It is appropriate to make interpretive reconstructions of the source of this sense of "entitlement" in the patient's early family development. Likewise, a patient consistently needing more time or more input from the therapist can sometimes come to see how excessive dependency needs have their psychological roots in childhood. I believe that these interpretations are most effective when couched in supportive and empathic rather than confrontational terms. The therapist can empathize with the psychological pain the person must have felt that necessitated their "needing" the "entitlement" approach to life. Similarly, people with hyperrage who come for treatment may have some intellectual understanding of the etiology of this rage, and they often have enough ego structure to modify their expression of it. As people's behavior becomes less demanding or abusive, their life experiences will generally become more gratifying and their sense of self-esteem will naturally increase.

Adding the transpersonal dimension to the therapy of people with character problems is effective in several ways. Spiritual systems, because they emphasize the sanctity of life in general and human lives in particular, generally have the effect of increasing self-esteem. Also, the emphasis on kindness and forgiveness that characterizes spiritual systems is often helpful to people with problems in the area of aggression. Of particular significance to individuals with character problems is the fact that spiritual traditions, in general, emphasize service and generosity. For people with problems in the area of empathy and/or respect for the rights and needs of others, this is often directly helpful.

My work with Pauline is especially instructive, since she appeared to have a very high level of ego organization and, in fact, was professionally quite successful. Her character pathology, which was subtle, prevented her from successfully maintaining any long-term, intimate relationships.

Case Study: Pauline

Pauline is a fifty-five-year-old advertising executive. She sought therapy because she realized she had an ongoing depression which, although mild, was chronically debilitating. She also had periodic rages and a hypercritical, sadomasochistic character style. Her need to control everyone in her environment was the primary cause of the failure of her two marriages. Pauline's parents had died when she was an infant, and she was brought up by an aunt who was cold, obsessional, and controlling. Although Pauline's earliest years seemed to be lacking in nurturance, she did not exhibit any visible ego boundary defects. She was intellectually and professionally very capable and had always managed to have friends, though she was hypercritical of herself and others. Her stubborn and defiant style, however, caused difficulties in intimate relationships. This seemed a reflection of the style she developed to deal with her aunt, who was punitive and rejecting.

Throughout her life, Pauline continued to set up relationships in which she felt victimized, repeating the pattern of how she perceived her early life. She would then feel angry and indignant about having been misused. Pauline longed for nurturance, but her stubborn and aggressive style of interacting often stood in the way of her receiving it. In my evaluation of this patient, I felt that, although she had experienced considerable trauma in the first few years of her life (reflected by her neediness and her defiance), she had a relatively strong and intact ego. I felt her difficulties lay mainly in the area of an overly rigid and demanding conscience and an identification with a style that was hypercritical, rejecting, and unempathic.

Because I felt Pauline's neediness and defiance were part of her character style and did not reflect pathology of ego boundaries, I began working with her using classical interpretive psychotherapy. In instances where Pauline was talking about childhood interchanges with her aunt that were difficult, I made what I felt were empathic comments such as, "That must have been really painful for you." When Pauline described current experiences where she felt criticized by either co-workers or friends, I would make interventions such as, "I'm sure this feels very painful for you, particularly given the sensitivity you have toward criticism from living with your aunt." In other words, I tried very hard to recognize her degree of discomfort and to avoid criticizing her for her sensitivity. Indeed, I hoped to validate her sensitivity by empathically referring to the pain in her life, which I felt was the source of this sensitivity. As Pauline felt more secure about my genuine concern and interest in her, her general demeanor seemed more relaxed. Whereas our early therapy sessions together had been characterized by a series of tirades describing the injustices that she'd been obliged to tolerate, her need to impress me with her degree of pain seemed to subside as I steadfastly provided empathetic support.

Eventually, Pauline began to be able to see that she derived pleasure from the sense of "righteous indignation" she felt in her victimized situation. She also began to observe that her feelings of self-pity were sometimes gratifying to her. As she began to see that the pleasure she derived from these painful situations was, in fact, a substitute for the pleasure she wished she had had in a nurturing and loving situation, she began to let go of this style. As her aggressive style lessened, the people around her then felt permitted (and encouraged) to provide her with more nurturance and acceptance, and this led to an apparent diminution of her neediness.

During the course of her therapy Pauline elected, on the advice of a friend, to take "est" training. She found many aspects of the training helpful. She seemed particularly impressed with the notion that straightforwardly telling the truth, which she characterized as "speaking up for oneself," could be done in a way that was assertive without being aggressive. This offered her the possibility of making constructive intentional character changes in her life rather than simply relinquishing her victim stance. She also was interested in the fact that the "est" system was presented as a psychological compendium of spiritual truths.

Because I was interested in Pauline's experience with "est" training and seemed supportive of it, she felt empowered to ask me about my own interest in spiritual practice. She was pleased to see that, rather than questioning her tentative expression of interest in meditation, I encouraged it. Further empowered by her "est"-training forthrightness, Pauline felt emboldened enough to ask me about my own meditative practice, and I told her I did Vipassana practice from the Buddhist tradition.

Pauline located an introductory one-day course in Vipassana practice and found it interesting and gratifying enough to sign up for a ten-day intensive retreat soon afterward. Sometimes beginning meditators find the deprivation of not talking and the intensity of the many hours of meditation practice to be a difficult experience; Pauline, however, found it nurturing and calming.

At our first therapy session following her ten-day retreat, Pauline was eager to report to me her breakthroughs of psychological understanding that had come as a result of meditation. As she spoke, I was able to appreciate the dual effects of a somewhat more relaxed mental state coupled with the Buddhist insights that I knew she had received as part of the didactic teaching that happens at retreats. Pauline reported that she had realized how much pain she experienced from her attachment to having things happen in a way that she controlled. She described to me periods of meditation in which she spontaneously remembered events in her life which she had experienced with tremendous suffering, appreciating now how that suffering had been intensified by her expectation that things would be better than they were. Although I was pleased with Pauline's new spiritual sophistication and happy she felt more emotional ease around these events, I was careful to assure her that her hopes had been reasonable ones. Children, I reminded her, ought to expect that things will go well for them. In other words, I hoped that her new spiritual sophistication would not short-circuit her need to experience her feelings honestly. I also did not want it to increase her tendency to be self-critical by overemphasizing the amount of pain that she had added to her situation. Paradoxically, although I often am hopeful that patients can divorce themselves from a critical style by seeing its self-defeating aspects, I was also eager that Pauline not use this awareness as fuel for more self-criticism.

As weeks went by, I began to feel reassured that the intellectual distance that Pauline's new understanding of suffering had provided had indeed begun to make her character style somewhat more ego-alien without demoralizing her. Even in those instances where she felt trapped in an opinion, and in her attachment to it, she could laughingly tolerate the painfulness of her situation. "I know it's true," she would say, "that I could be free of this suffering if I just let go of my attachment, but I can't."

During her Vipassana retreat Pauline had learned *metta* (lovingkindness) meditation. She had found that recitation of the intent to forgive herself and others made her feel better even though, as she said, "I don't really feel sincere about it." It was difficult for her to understand why focusing on thoughts of forgiveness should dissipate anger, especially if she felt the anger to be "righteously motivated." However, she admitted that the meditation did seem to work, and so she continued to practice it.

The retreat was pivotal in Pauline's experience with therapy for a number of reasons. She found that both the calm of the retreat atmosphere and the concentration of the practice were nurturing. She discovered that the forgiveness meditation decreased her feelings of anger as they came up and also made her hopeful that she might be less troubled by angry feelings in the future. In addition, she was buoyed up by her ongoing experiences after the retreat, which continued to confirm that, as her opinions and expectations lessened, her suffering likewise abated.

One further offshoot of her stay at the meditation retreat was that Pauline became interested in reading spiritual literature. She wanted to know more about how meditation works. She found that she very much enjoyed reading about people's spiritual journeys, particularly the lives of saints, gurus, and famous meditation teachers. Because many of these stories emphasize forgiveness, I think this reading had the effect of modulating Pauline's overly rigid conscience. Through reading about various spiritual teachers, she was able to identify with new role models, learning more skillful and loving ways of interacting with others. Pursuing her interest in Vipassana meditation, Pauline felt accepted by teachers whom she esteemed, and this fulfilled both the mirroring and idealizing aspects of relational development.

Pauline continued to attend retreats on a regular basis and after some time began to make tentative friendships with other regular retreatants. At the same time that she ended therapy, about one year after her first retreat, she joined a meditation group that met once a week. This group of seven met without a teacher, and Pauline enjoyed the experience of feeling a peer with the other meditators. The group meditated together and then discussed how their meditation practice was active in their day-to-day lives. Pauline reported to me at our last meeting together that she felt that she was well-regarded and recognized in the group as a person with valuable spiritual understanding.

I am including the following summary of my work with Robert because he felt that all of the transpersonal additions to his therapy, techniques he'd practiced or tried to be interested in because of my interest in them, were valueless. Indeed, although he dabbled briefly in reading spiritual literature, he always remained severely critical of its irrationality. Also, although he attended several

Vipassana seminars and retreats and found them pleasant and relaxing, he never built up much interest in practicing the meditation itself and never followed through on the practice apart from the retreats. Nevertheless, it was my impression that this exposure to transpersonal value systems, through his reading experiences and through his meditation experiences, was having a salubrious effect on him, as if by osmosis.

I believe that the traditional, psychoanalytically oriented, interpretive technique we worked with produced some character change. In addition, the values of the spiritual tradition, providing new role models for identification, also helped effect change. Each modality seemed to enhance the other. The success of the interpretive therapy built a strong therapeutic alliance between Robert and myself, and his respect for my opinions then led him to consider the transpersonal dimension. Although he did not embrace a particular spiritual practice, his consideration of spiritual paths highlighted for him most clearly his areas of characterological problems. These were then more readily available for discussion and interpretation in the therapy setting.

Case Study: Robert

Robert was a forty-nine-year-old dentist who had been married for twenty-two years and had two teenage sons. He sought therapy for his ongoing depression and his preoccupying fear of dying. His concern with financial security caused him, in spite of his strong financial situation, to work to excess. Robert's parents had been rigid, ungenerous people, very harsh in their expectations. Although Robert had been an outstanding student, his parents had always been critical of him. They could have easily afforded to send him to college, but they refused to do so. Their refusal was based on their opinion that college cost too much money. The message Robert had gotten from this refusal, which was characteristic of his parents, was that he was not worthy of their interest and effort. I believe this was the foundation of his predicament in life. He was working excessively hard, never feeling that he had sufficient supplies, resenting the fact that he needed to do everything by himself, and basically not trusting anyone else.

In evaluating Robert, I felt he did not have any problems with ego boundary defects. Rather, I felt that he had major emotional fixations in the early stages of psychological development and that his major problem was an overpunitive superego and an ego ideal that was unrealistic and ungratifying.

I undertook an interpretive approach with Robert, couching all of my interpretations in what I felt was an empathic context. His early life traumas soon represented themselves in the transference relationship. My relative silence led Robert to feel I was being critical of him. He felt, and was able to express, his fear that I was treating him only because I was interested in his money. My consistent efforts were to empathize with the pain he must have experienced at feeling that his parents did not find him worthy enough of attention and subsequently, as an adult, that others did not find him worthy of their attention. Each time this conflict presented itself and was empathically noted, Robert seemed to have considerable relief of tension.

Robert's tendency to criticize both himself and others became less severe as we worked together, I believe through the internalization of what he felt to be my tolerance and empathy. I supposed that this was a result of his sense of being nourished by his relationship with me, which he experienced as very supportive. Because Robert valued me, he became interested in what he perceived, through our discussions, to be my interests.

An ongoing problem for Robert was his fear of death; he was preoccupied by it. He read some books I recommended that present the transpersonal view of death and dying. He did not find these particularly useful. He was not satisfied with the idea that spirit was eternal—he wanted ego and personality to be eternal.

Although he had only the most superficial knowledge of transpersonal theory, he criticized its "irrationality." On the basis of the considerable respect Robert had for me, he took classes in Vipassana meditation and even attended several retreats. He was not especially drawn to meditation, and the strangeness of the retreat atmosphere was disconcerting to him. But his esteem for me and his knowledge of my interest and faith in this practice probably led him to maintain some hope that it would be helpful to him.

Perhaps the most important effect of Robert's attendance at the Vipassana meditation seminars was that they gave him another perspective about what is valuable. He admired the teachers, who seemed to him, in addition to being very intelligent, to be empathic, tolerant, kind, and self-assured without being self-aggrandizing. In the Theravada tradition, mindfulness retreats are available to retreatants at a minimal charge that covers only the cost of room and board. None of the money paid at retreats goes to teachers, who offer their teaching services freely, without promise of compensation. Although voluntary gifts of financial compensation are accepted by teachers, they are optional and entirely voluntary. Since Robert's experience was with parents who were miserly in terms of affection and supplies, this experience of being "given to" by strangers was powerfully transformative. He was also impressed with the other meditators, who generally seemed more interested in spiritual development than in power, fame, or money, which had been his parents' principal preoccupations. He began to recognize and lament the fact that, although he had achieved financial and professional security, he was still unhappy and uneasy.

There were many instances in the therapy when I felt that perhaps I had been remiss in urging Robert to do transpersonal reading or attend meditation seminars. He himself dismissed his experiences with both of these as being worthless. However, I began to see considerable changes in him. He gradually became less self-critical and much less critical of others. He began to worry less about his financial status. Sometimes he teased me about not being worried anymore since, as he said, "I know the cosmos is taking care of me." He was playfully mocking what he felt to be my transpersonal stance. At the same time, I believed he hoped it was true that the cosmos is benevolent, and his mockery was a way of defending himself from knowing how strongly he wished it were true. I thought Robert's need to have the cosmos a caring place reflected the fact that his early life situation had been non-caring and non-nurturing. He had experienced his parents' care of him as being solely an obligation and a duty, certainly not an act of love. His exposure to transpersonal concepts through his readings and his retreat experiences had transmitted to him, by association or by identification, a more helpful outlook on life.

As therapy with Robert continued, he began to place more value on his family relationships. And as his priorities and values changed, he was able to give up his excessive preoccupation with financial success and security.

I felt that most of these changes came about because of the strong, personal positive relationship Robert had with me and the identification he was able to make with the point of view that he knew I held. In other words, he was able to substitute my value system for his previous value system, one that he had developed through identification with his parents. I think it was healing to him, in terms of his early deprivation, to have me "think enough of him" to encourage him to attend a meditation retreat, an activity that I myself participated in. To put this in Self Psychology terminology, Robert had idealized me and correctly felt that I esteemed him (mirroring).

The work with both Pauline and Robert provides examples of situations in which interpretive psychotherapy is facilitated and reinforced by the addition of a transpersonal value system which, through providing new models for identification, modifies character style. Although Pauline showed considerable interest in transpersonal techniques and Robert essentially eschewed them, in both cases basic values of the spiritual tradition seemed to have rubbed off on them.

It is instructive and valuable to acknowledge that people need not actually feel psychologically ready to let go of attachments or to spontaneously practice generosity or kindness. Yet it appears that spending time in a milieu where these are the valued character traits can, in itself, effect a change. That is to say, I believe it is possible for a person to practice generosity or kindness out of a desire to imitate an esteemed person who, it is hoped and expected, will mirror back a sense of caring. I also believe that the practice of these traits, which leads to more harmonious and gratifying relationships, with a concomitant increase in self-esteem, does in itself promote healing of psychological damage.

In my description of my treatment of Ned, it will become clear that although we had little time available for significant interpretive psychotherapy, the affirming nature of my interactions with him, combined with the effects of his daily practice of the principles of *A Course in Miracles*, led to profound characterological changes. These in turn produced an increase in happiness and love in his life.

Case Study: Ned

Ned was a fifty-one-year-old junior executive who consulted me because of a lifelong feeling of worthlessness that he saw as currently a component of his failing marriage. He came from a large Protestant family of German origin. As the middle child of seven boys and girls, Ned had received most of his care and nurturance from his siblings. He described his mother as "prim and proper," a schoolteacher who valued neatness and felt that "children should be seen but not heard." Ned said that compliments were reserved only for those people who earned lots of money. Ned himself volunteered that he had probably gone into the banking industry as a reflection of his desire for parental esteem. He said that although his mother was quite straightlaced, she was "a closet alcoholic" and was frequently unavailable to her children.

Ned's father was an executive in his uncle's business. He was cruel and sadistic to Ned, using money as his primary mode of relating. In addition, he conveyed to his son his view that women were worthless except as sexual objects. Throughout his marriage to Ned's mother, Ned's father had many affairs that were openly acknowledged by the family. Ned's mother stayed in the marriage because she was too frightened to leave, and his father stayed because he could comfortably benefit from the status of being married while carrying on his extramarital liaisons.

All of Ned's brothers and sisters had made very strong identifications with their parents' character pathologies. I believe that lack of nurturance in childhood was a primary reason for Ned's lifelong struggle against obsessive overeating, especially when feeling under stress. Although overeating was only one of the symptoms Ned mentioned to me in our first meeting, he was also aware that his frequent rage attacks and ongoing antagonistic stance contributed to his marriage difficulties.

In Ned's childhood home, there had been minimal Christian observance. Holiday activities were maintained but church attendance was infrequent. There was no family discussion of Christian values or indeed of any values.

Ned wanted very much to be admired by his wife and his three sons and he'd worked very hard hoping to gain their approval. However, all of the values that had been approved in his childhood family, especially those of amassing large sums of money, led his wife and sons to scorn him. Ned had had several affairs throughout his thirty years of marriage. Apart from his father, who both frightened and awed him, Ned had no conventional adult role models. Although he had reasonable financial success in his business career, he felt that he was a total failure in his life.

Prior to our meeting, Ned had nothing but ridicule and contempt for anything spiritual or religious. This recapitulated the views held by his family of origin. His wife was a devout Catholic whom Ned had mocked throughout their marriage for her religious beliefs.

I liked Ned from our very first meeting, and I believe he felt that. Because frequent meetings and intense psychotherapy were not possible, I felt that the infrequent meetings we could have would be leveraged if Ned had a spiritual practice we could both relate to. Even though he ridiculed Christian belief systems and religious practices, I felt Ned might benefit from them. He was nominally a Christian. I thought that *A Course in Miracles* would be of great ancillary help to Ned both as an affirming, accepting spiritual practice and as a guide or role model for how to approach his life from a position of caring and forgiveness. I also thought that *A Course in Miracles* might be a particularly appropriate vehicle for Ned given his stubborn character style. A prominent theme with him was that of having been "pushed around" by the others in his family throughout his early life. *A Course in Miracles* is a book that can be opened and closed at the reader's will and therefore does not raise the transference problems of being pushed around by another human being.

Ned's immediate, positive response to working with the meditation exercises and text of *A Course in Miracles* was one of the most dramatic I have ever seen. The non-expression of anger and the practice of forgiveness became the cornerstones of Ned's new approach to life. When he began therapy, he was plagued by feelings of guilt over his past uncaring behavior toward his wife and sons. Over the next six months, working with the *Course*, he began to forgive himself. He was able to reflect that, although he felt badly about what he had done in the past, there was no way to change what had already happened, and he decided that he could now best use his energy by focusing on the creation of better relationships with his wife and children. Likewise, he was at last able to see the various cruelties that his parents and siblings had inflicted on him as having been beyond their conscious control, and his obsessive angry thoughts about them subsided. As Ned's style changed from angry to pleasant and caring, his family did respond to him with more affection. He felt more relaxed. He reported less obsessive preoccupation with eating and discovered that he was eating less, losing weight, looking better, and feeling proud of himself.

Ned's psychopathology could be understood as a "healthy" identification in his childhood with pathologic family values. His low self-esteem could certainly be understood from the point of view of Self Psychology as being the reflection of the total lack of empathic response toward him from his parents. Because of his combative and stubborn style, it would have been hard for Ned to develop and sustain a depth relationship with another human being who might serve as his new ego ideal. Working with *A Course in Miracles*, Ned was able to relate to Jesus as an ego ideal. It was somewhat ironic that he should become sincerely engaged in religious practice, considering the long-term mocking stance he had had about his wife's religious devotion. Even as he practiced *A Course in Miracles,* Ned maintained that the *Course* was a more sophisticated religious path than the "regular" religious pursuits of his wife. Perhaps Ned needs to overinflate his religious path as a way to bolster his own fundamentally poor self-esteem as well as a way to avoid apologizing for yet one more act of inconsiderateness in his past.

In spiritual communities there are a fair number of individuals who (when they come to us for help) like to keep the clinician's focus on their "spirituality," thus avoiding letting themselves or others discover that they are using the "spiritual life" to hide many inadequacies of their life. I call this "taking a spiritual shortcut." For example, not infrequently I'll meet someone who will be hiding his or her inability to develop intimate relationships behind the oft-quoted spiritual goal of "not being attached." It is crucial that the transpersonal therapist not be seduced into the exciting area of the spiritual pursuit, thereby missing what is more important now for the patient, i.e., resolving the issues that have resulted from psychological traumas inflicted early in life.

This may also show up in patients who want to focus on dream work in order to access their spiritual life. Again, it is important here to honor the validity and importance of this type of activity, but not as a replacement for, nor at the cost of, working to resolve and work through early-life psychological problems. In fact, what happens is that the astute transpersonal therapist keeps focusing on the earlier material while, at the same time, going along with the patient on the spiritual journey. This material is described on a theoretical level by Ken Wilber in his paper "Pre/Trans Fallacy" (see Chapter 2, p. 40).

Chapter 7

The Transpersonal Treatment of
Neurotic Illness

ACCORDING TO A CLASSICAL psychoanalytic framework, neurotic disorders derive from intrapsychic conflict between instinctual sexual and aggressive drives and an emerging conscience or superego. The traditional formulation of the etiology of these conflicts is that they begin in children somewhere between the ages of three and six. The traditional view of the particular intrapsychic conflict involved is that the child needs to resolve and integrate forbidden sexual and aggressive feelings toward the parents. A recent shift in emphasis has evolved among some psychoanalytically oriented therapists, based on the work of Heinz Kohut. It was Kohut's hypothesis that, although neurotic disorders do reflect the non-resolution of the nuclear family conflict, this non-resolution can actually be traced to an incomplete consolidation of a sense of self at an earlier age, stemming from a failure of empathy. It was his conclusion that individuals who developed a strong sense of self, through adequate nurturance and empathy in the first few years of life, were able to deal with sexual and aggressive strivings without their becoming a problem.

If real human development were as neat as academic and theoretical formulations, the emergence (and hoped-for resolution) of this family triangle situation would come about after all the previous levels of normal psychosexual development had been completed. That is to say, in healthy psychological development it is presumed that the normal first-year need for nurturance and second-

and third-year needs for development of self-control and a sense of personal autonomy would have been satisfactorily completed by the time a child entered the oedipal phase of development. If that were true, it would be theoretically possible for a three- or four-year-old child to deal with the newly emerging social and sexual dilemmas with optimum psychological energy. What is probably the actual situation is that most individuals entering the oedipal phase of development (and indeed continuing on throughout their lives) have unresolved areas of conflict resulting from minor fixations at earlier stages of development, which continue to make demands on the psyche. These fixations may manifest in terms of a lifelong feeling of need for nurturance, lifelong concerns over self-control and the control of others, and perhaps some impairment of the self-esteem system. In working with people who are essentially neurotic, it is assumed that these fixations are of minor significance and that their sense of ego boundary is not damaged, as would be the case in individuals with more primitive levels of ego organization.

Most traditional psychoanalytically oriented psychotherapy aims for the resolution of conflict through the reactivation, within the relationship between therapist and patient, of the oedipal conflicts. The hoped-for result is that the uncovering of unconscious wishes and fears, when confronted in a non-threatening setting, will lead to the resolution of these fears and the satisfactory expression of libidinal drives under the aegis of the now more mature ego. In this framework, interventions and interpretations usually focus on the drives and fears that stem from the oedipal era. Therapists who favor the viewpoint of Heinz Kohut and the Self Psychologists would emphasize interpretations and interventions that focus on failures of empathy and nurturance in pre-oedipal and oedipal development.

In my own experience, I have found that differentiating these two types of responses is arbitrary, misleading, and unnecessary. All responses, including interpretive ones, can be conveyed in terms that are empathic. Indeed, I believe that psychological responses need to be expressed empathically in order to be heard and assimilated. Effective responses are those that emphasize the fear that the patient, as a child, must have had in reaction to experiences that were overwhelming. Such responses acknowledge

what was true, but more importantly, I believe, they heal the rup-
tured sense of empathy that is the fundamental source of psychological pain.

I have presented my view of the treatment of neurotic disorders in some detail because I believe it serves as a rationale and
an explanation for the effectiveness of Vipassana meditation for
individuals with neurotic problems. Vipassana meditation, especially in a retreat milieu, recreates many aspects of intense depth
psychotherapy. Being surrounded by supportive meditators and
caring teachers in a setting that emphasizes kindness, calm, and
non-harming is similar to the sense of being cared for in the calm,
reliable, attentive atmosphere of a good psychotherapeutic relationship. The practice of mindfulness, basic and fundamental to
Vipassana practice, leads to the development of a sense of balanced
observing awareness. This parallels the sense of balanced observing ego that can be developed, through free association, in working
with a skilled therapist. The increasing ability, through meditation
practice, to experience an entire range of memories, feelings, and
sensations with a sense of equanimity reflects the desired goal of
psychotherapy to acknowledge, understand, and integrate one's
unconscious processes.

In this chapter, I present four summaries of psychotherapy
work with individuals who seemed primarily to have neurotic difficulties. The first three case studies demonstrate how the practice of
Vipassana meditation in conjunction with traditional psychotherapy facilitated the therapy. Although all of these people were uncomfortable enough to seek psychotherapy, they had intact, well-functioning egos and were professionally quite successful. Each one had
significant fixations stemming from lack of nurturance in early
development. For one person, the intensive retreat situation was
experienced as nurturing; for another, it was a deprivation; and for
another, the setting was not particularly significant. For one person,
the concentration practice led to a certain amount of calm and the
development of a more dispassionate observing ego, which facilitated traditional psychotherapy. In two other situations, the retreat
practice itself led to a breakdown of ego repression, producing significant unconscious, forgotten, and repressed material with its

associated affect, which was later available to be worked on in continuing psychotherapy.

The fourth case summary describes the meshing of psychotherapy with spiritual practice in a slightly different way. This individual came to me for therapy because of difficulties he was experiencing in his spiritual practice.

Case Study: Matthew

Matthew began therapy when he was thirty years old. He was a high school administrator, unmarried, who sought therapy for low self-esteem, loneliness, and a sense of isolation. He felt that sexuality was an area of conflict for him. He was aware of being hypercritical of himself and expressed a generalized, vague dissatisfaction with life.

Matthew had been the only child of parents who he felt could love him only if he were "perfect." His parents, both professional people, had very high aspirations for their child and were supportive of his academic goals. Perhaps it was this very supportiveness, which he experienced as intrusive and demanding, that had made him feel throughout his life that his parents, particularly his mother, were not empathic to his needs. It is difficult to know, in retrospect, whether Matthew's parents were actually excessively demanding of him or whether it was Matthew himself who set especially high expectations for himself academically because he knew this was what his mother admired most about his father. He acknowledged having always felt a sense of competition between himself and his father for the affection of his mother. My evaluation of Matthew was that his major conflicts were around oedipal issues.

My therapeutic work with him was primarily interpretive. My hope was that by exposing his oedipal wishes and the defenses against these wishes, there would be a lessening of that part of his self-criticism that came from oedipal guilt. I also assumed, since I genuinely liked Matthew and felt that he liked me, that he would regard our relationship as an empathic one, and that this would serve to heal the deprivations that were the underpinnings of his oedipal conflicts. I suggested he take some classes in Vipassana meditation and consider attending a meditation retreat. I decided it would be helpful to him in terms of gaining some awareness of his hypercritical thought patterns. I assumed that as he became more aware of these thought patterns they would lessen. I also believed that in a group setting he would experience a sense of being nurtured and cared for in a non-harming, benevolent environment, and that this would heal some of his early trauma.

Matthew found participating in Vipassana meditation retreats immediately beneficial and continued this practice on his own. He attended several week-long or ten-day retreats a year, depending on what he could schedule into his school vacation time. As I had expected, he experienced the calm, tolerant, and supportive atmosphere of the retreat situation as being personally nurturing. Even though these retreats are conducted in silence, with minimal interpersonal interaction, the presence and the demeanor of the people around him reinforced his own efforts. One philosophical tenet of Buddhism, of which Vipassana practice is a particular technique, is that our basic nature is one of kindness and compassion, and Matthew felt especially soothed and reassured learning these teachings through the talks or the meditation practice instructions.

In therapy, Matthew seemed to improve dramatically. I felt this improvement was particularly facilitated by his participation in Vipassana practice. I further believed his improvement could be understood from the Kohutian point of view of the healing of the self system, as well as the more classical view of the resolution of oedipal conflict. From the standpoint of the Self Psychologists, the experiences Matthew had both in psychotherapy and at meditation retreats were beneficial at the level of impairment to the self system. My belief was that a large part of his difficulties had come from his sense of a lack of empathy on the part of his parents for his particular needs. This lack of empathy, a non-affirmation of the child's importance or specialness, undermined the sense of secure identity that would have enabled Matthew, as a child, to cope with his oedipal strivings and fears. I felt that this failure of early empathy was addressed in therapy, (more in context than in content) in the bond that I understood existed between Matthew and myself. I knew he viewed me as being interested and genuinely concerned for him. I felt it was important to him that I suggest he participate in Vipassana retreats, because he knew it was a practice I did myself and this represented my seeing him as an equal. His participation in the retreats, his sense of being included with people he admired, had the further beneficial effect of nourishing his self-esteem.

The more traditional aspect of Matthew's therapy, working through the defenses against his forbidden drives, was also part of the healing process. In classical interpretive psychotherapy, the therapist helps the patient see the way in which he or she defends against the awareness of certain repressed strivings and wishes. Although these defenses might have seemed necessary early in childhood, they are irrelevant to the adult, and it is the therapist's task to help the patient see this so that he or she can become more open and free of anxiety.

It is, of course, difficult to evaluate quantitatively exactly how much Matthew's meditation practice enhanced his ability to participate in this form of psychotherapy. It is my feeling, however, that the increased calm he was able to maintain as a result of his meditation practice, along with the heightened sense of observing awareness, improved his ability to work well in classical interpretive therapy.

As Matthew's interest in Vipassana meditation practice increased, he also became interested in reading Buddhist literature. This would have been a predictable response, since he is essentially an academic and a scholar. He found that concepts such as the essential unity of all consciousness and the basic purity and goodness of spirit were both reassuring and self-affirming.

It has been my experience, in working with Matthew and with others who, like him, have difficulties with self-esteem, that even when these concepts of essential purity, goodness, or oneness of spirit are only intellectual concepts (as opposed to experientially validated truths), they have a positive effect. They serve to heighten self-esteem and lessen self-criticalness. As Matthew's therapy progressed and he felt more spontaneous and less inhibited, he was able to develop more gratifying interpersonal relationships. This new social ease also served to continue to heighten his increasing sense of self-esteem.

My work with Bruce is a fairly dramatic example of two points I want to emphasize. The first is the need, both in initially evaluating a patient and later on as the treatment proceeds, to be open to reassessing diagnostic formulations and treatment plans. In this instance, Bruce's presenting complaints seemed principally of an existential nature, and his ego functioning seemed very solid. When he began to practice Vipassana meditation, a practice I suggested to him as a possible source of spiritual insights, he experienced symptoms that reflected difficulties at both neurotic and pre-neurotic levels. This case summary also demonstrates that it is possible to move from affect uncovered in meditation retreats to insights worked through in psychotherapy and that these psychotherapeutic gains may then lead to further meditative practice and insights.

Case Study: Bruce

Bruce was a forty-nine-year-old engineer with three grown children, who came to see me specifically because he knew, through a mutual friend, that I was involved with transpersonal therapy. Fifteen years previously, he had undertaken several years of classical, psychoanalytically oriented psychotherapy for problems of anxiety and lack of self-confidence, which had seemed, at the time, to be successful. His symptoms had then decreased, and his marriage and family relationships had become more comfortable. His career was successful and he was relatively affluent. A symptom, however, that had continued throughout the intervening years, but which had not been severe enough to motivate him to seek treatment, was a low level of sadness and melancholia.

He sought treatment with me because he was troubled by the idea that his life was frivolous or trivial, that it was not sufficiently meaningful, and that it was passing by very quickly. He found himself increasingly preoccupied with thoughts of death and dying. His upcoming fiftieth birthday felt to him like a landmark. His father, a gentle but passive man, had died one year previously. His mother, an angry, hypercritical woman, had died several years before that. Bruce felt he had become more depressed about not finding abiding meaning in his life after his father's recent death. With both parents gone, he felt himself to be "next in line." Bruce said that although his parents, particularly his mother, had been practicing Catholics, their religious beliefs had always seemed superficial to him. As soon as he had been able to do so, he had stopped going to church. However, since childhood he had been aware of a continuing interest in mystical speculation about the meaning of life. *Lost Horizon*, by James Hilton, had been a favorite book of his.

Prior to coming to see me, Bruce had attended several weekend workshops on higher consciousness and briefly studied with a Silva Mind Control group. He had been particularly impressed with the instances of extrasensory perception or healing that happened in these groups. Paranormal phenomena were especially startling to him since, as an engineer, he had a scientific background. Rather than rejecting these phenomena as impossible, he found them exciting. In evaluating Bruce, I thought at first that his difficulties were mainly of an existential nature, something like a "midlife crisis." The fact that he was approaching a midlife age milestone and the recent death of his father seemed to point to this conclusion. He did tell me, as I took the careful, developmental history that I always record in meeting new patients, that his mother had required three months to recuperate from complications surrounding his birth. During this time, Bruce had been kept in the relative isolation of a nursery, separated from his mother. I suspected that this had something to do with his melancholia, but since he had minimized this symptom and since this issue had apparently not been a prominent one in his earlier psychotherapy, I underestimated its significance. Also, because he did not mention any particular marriage difficulties and had been married for seventeen years, I concluded, somewhat prematurely and erroneously, that he did not have significant energy tied up in unresolved oedipal conflicts.

I began treatment with Bruce operating on the assumption that his difficulties were mainly age-related and existential. Because he was only a few years younger than I, we were able to discuss the fact that questions of life and death and meaning are normal ones for people at midlife. I was also able to suggest to him several books in the area of Transpersonal Psychology, especially the work of Ken Wilber, which I felt might be helpful to him. Because Bruce sensed my personal interest in the issues that seemed most central to him at the time, we established an empathic bond and consolidated a good working alliance.

Aware of his Christian background, I suggested he read *A Course in Miracles*. He was very enthusiastic about it. It reassured him that the spiritual search, the pursuit of meaning that had been a lifelong interest of his, was a valid one. Because the *Course* emphasizes the practice of forgiveness, Bruce found that working with it had the effect of lessening both his self-criticism and his criticism of others. Both of these traits had been internalized through his identification with his excessively critical mother. It was in this curious, roundabout way that his hypercritical nature was first mentioned and became a factor in his therapy. I had suggested *A Course in Miracles* for its spiritual answers to his existential questions. His spontaneous reporting that it had attenuated his judgmental thinking led to my discovery that his hypercritical nature had been a continuing source of friction between Bruce and his wife. Although their marriage was indeed stable, I began to suspect more problems in the area of intimate relationship, stemming from oedipal conflict, than I had previously imagined.

I suggested to Bruce that he try Vipassana meditation. He attended some weekend workshops and then began to attend longer retreats. Initially, the primary benefit he derived from the practice was the reassurance that he was doing something constructive to deal with the need for meaning in his life. He found that being in the company of people who had this common goal was very helpful to him. He thought the rigors of the long retreat situation (the silence, the hours of sitting still, and the unusual diet) made him feel a great bond of empathy with all the other meditators, along with an increased sense of compassion. Self Psychologists might see this peer-group identification as an example of the twinship or alter ego aspect of relationship. Bruce reported that this practice, along with his continued use of *A Course in Miracles,* was continuing to soften his hypercritical style. As his style changed, his relationship with his wife and sons began to improve, and he felt sufficiently well to discontinue therapy.

He continued his Vipassana practice. Approximately a year after we had terminated his therapy, he resumed therapy as a result of what had occurred during a ten-day Vipassana retreat he had just attended. Although ample food is provided at these retreats, Bruce had decided on this particular occasion to eat very little. This was motivated partially by his awareness that being somewhat overweight all of his life reflected some lack of self-discipline, and he thought this would be a good opportunity to change this trait. Also, he knew that eating a lot causes sleepiness, and his plan to eat very little was an attempt to improve his alertness during meditation. As the days passed, Bruce felt himself to be unusually hungry. He realized that the degree of hunger he felt was disproportionate, since he was eating, and that it probably related more to the idea that he was depriving himself than to actual deprivation.

After several days of feeling hungry, Bruce found that his mind had become flooded with fantasies about breasts and his craving for them. The fantasies were totally ego alien, primitive, and represented his seeing women just as breasts or feeders. At some points, he experienced anxiety whenever he walked near or sat next to an attractive woman, as the thought crossed his mind that he would like to touch her breasts. His affect fluctuated from anxiety to unhappiness to despair. After many days, during which time he was unable to stop the fantasies, he had a lengthy, happy dream of a reunion with a healthy and nurturing mother. Although the dream seemed to bring an end to his fantasies and his anxiety, it was followed by a deep state of sadness and melancholy, which Bruce continued to experience after returning home from this retreat. It was this experience that prompted him to come back to therapy. Although his dream had been quite short, his associations to it were manifold and poignant and provided an enormous amount of material to be worked through in therapy.

His lifelong sense of mild depression and melancholia, which during the deprivation experience of the retreat had escalated into feelings of intense need, could be traced back to many instances of deprivation in his early life. Although Bruce never directly remembered his separation from his mother, he recalled with great sadness the anecdotes that he had heard from early childhood about his birth and his mother's illness. He had spent the first three months of his life in the nursery at a Catholic orphanage, while his mother recuperated from her post-partum complications sufficiently to resume care of him. Stories that had always seemed remote to him, describing how the nursery was run on a very strict feeding schedule, that the babies cried all the time, and that his crying was the loudest of all, now struck him as depressing and very sad. What he did remember more directly were his feelings of dismay and despair throughout his childhood whenever his mother recounted the story of his birth, because it seemed to him that she was implying that he had caused her post-partum complications and life-threatening illness.

Another aspect that became clear at this point in Bruce's therapy was that, although his mother had been somewhat overindulgent in food preparation, (perhaps setting the pattern for his lifelong overweight problem), she had been underindulgent in giving compliments or reassurance. Indeed, her harsh and hypercritical nature, at the same time that it was a deprivation of nurturance, was also the source of Bruce's low self-esteem, as well as his hypercritical judgment of himself and others.

A final significant, symbolic aspect of Bruce's dream was that this vision of himself in the dream was as a boy, approximately eleven years old. This was the age he had been when his younger sister was born. In terms of Bruce's own nurturing, an area that he now felt and acknowledged to have been deficient throughout his childhood, the birth of his sister had been the final blow. He remembered feeling intensely lonesome during the week his mother was hospitalized for his sister's birth. Even her return home was not comforting to him, since she was preoccupied with caring for the baby.

As Bruce continued to work through these memories and their affect, he was increasingly able to identify the roots of his own character style. During his childhood, during periods of his mother's physical or emotional absence from him, he had comforted himself by staying at home, reading fairy tales, listening to music, and eating, especially sweets, to make himself feel contented. His melancholy mood had kept him aloof from friends. As Bruce recognized elements of this character style that had continued into his adulthood and as he relived the deprivation experiences of his childhood in his therapy, his style began to change. He became more cheerful and less melancholy. His problems with overeating decreased. He noticed that as time passed his more cheerful mood at work led to more stimulating and gratifying friendships with his colleagues. His questions about the meaning of life diminished. It seemed clear that, although part of his initial concern about the need for a meaning of life probably did (and still does) reflect a real transpersonal concern, a considerable portion of his sense of lack of meaning dated back to those experiences of deprivation throughout his infancy and childhood.

Approximately six months after Bruce resumed therapy, he attended another ten-day Vipassana retreat. He recognized, with pleasure, a woman he had been aware of on several previous retreats, whom he had found to be quite attractive.

He found that he was spending a great deal of time in erotic fantasies about her. As the retreat progressed, he became aware of the fact, from various subtle clues, that she was involved in a relationship with another man at the retreat. He began to have, in addition to the erotic fantasies, disarmingly startling fantasies about aggressively attacking the man she was involved with and simultaneous fears that this man would attack him. It is important to make clear that throughout this entire period of fears and fantasies, Bruce had no personal acquaintance with either the woman or the man and did not even know their names. He was aware of the bizarreness of his preoccupation, given the fact that he had a wife at home toward whom he felt positive and committed feelings. On the one hand, he was aware that his fantasies and fears were somewhat ludicrous; on the other hand, as he shared silent dish-washing chores with his nameless male "competitor," he felt genuinely alarmed and threatened.

The combination of Bruce's psychotherapy and his meditation training had helped him develop a fairly strong observing ego. He was able to make use of the fantasy experienced at the retreat to begin to recover in psychotherapy memories of his own childhood and his rivalry with his father for the affections of his mother. He had told me at the outset of our work together that he had become aware of some rivalrous feelings toward his father in his earlier psychotherapy and that he considered that these feelings had been dealt with. The degree of affect that had been present in his fantasies in the meditation retreat, both the erotic, libidinal desires toward a particular attractive woman and the aggressive feelings toward the man he determined was her relationship partner, was a distinct surprise to him. Further psychotherapeutic exploration brought to light the fact that, although his mother was not emotionally nurturing toward him, she had, in fact, been somewhat seductive to him, especially in areas of food overindulgence. His father had been a mild and passive man. Bruce came to realize in his therapy that he had wished when he was a child that his father had been stronger. This would have served as a buffer and as a reassurance against his own libidinal desires toward his mother. It also would have protected him from his mother's anger and criticism.

The unique atmosphere of the Vipassana retreat allowed Bruce to recreate the same constellation of transference wishes and fears that one normally recreates in therapy. Out of all the participants in the retreat, he was able to select male and female examples who represented for him his own family situation. Because he was, as a result of his previous psychotherapy, fairly psychologically sophisticated, he was aware at all times of the inappropriateness of his affect and the fact that it must point to issues of more significant meaning. As he continued to work out these oedipal issues and rivalries in his therapy, his sexual enthusiasm increased and his sexual response became warmer and more spontaneous. With this change, his relationship with his wife became more affectionate and gratifying. As his intimate life became more gratifying, his questions about meaning and purpose in life seemed less significant. It was clear that although he had not answered these questions they seemed to consume less of his psychological energy. I felt, just as I had with the issue of basic nurturance, that a fair portion of Bruce's previous preoccupation with "existential" problems had been a defensive maneuver to keep him from dealing with unresolved issues around the matter of interpersonal relationship and intimacy.

Bruce's relationship with his wife, although it had always been cordial, seemed imbued with a new-found excitement. He discovered himself to be much more spontaneous in his expressions of affection. Although he had passed his fiftieth birthday, the event that had previously loomed ominously before him, he felt enthusiastic about his family relationships, his work, and, in addition, the possibility of further gains through continued spiritual practice. Although Bruce discontinued his therapy at this point, he has remained in contact with me on an infrequent basis and seems to continue to consolidate the gains he made in therapy.

The preceding case summary, and the one that now follows, both reflect dramatically the specific way in which intense Vipassana meditation practice may be interpolated into traditional psychotherapy. Although the nurturing aspect of the retreat situation, the calm and secure atmosphere and the warmth and compassion of the teachers are, of course, significant to individuals at all levels of psychosexual development, they are less important to people with well-developed ego structures than they seem to be to people with more fragile psychological development. For individuals with sound ego development, particularly individuals who have experience with psychotherapy and are familiar with the concept of watching and reporting one's own mental processes, the retreat situation seems an ideal setting in which to deepen their introspective awareness. The concentration practice fundamental to Vipassana meditation produces the calm that facilitates the development of an observing awareness. The concentration practice also promotes equanimity, which allows the awareness to stay steady and focused, even when the experiences it observes, either mental or physical, are unpleasant. I have seen that even in initial practice, people with essentially secure and strong levels of ego development often begin to uncover forgotten, repressed, or "forbidden" material. This is very much a parallel of what happens in intense psychotherapy, such as psychoanalysis. The combination of focused attention and decreased input of stimuli destabilizes ego defenses that have previously served to keep these memories or feelings hidden. My sense is, furthermore, that it is the combination of the personal calm and steadiness of mind in a supportive retreat environment that makes the emergence of this material tolerable.

Case Study: Mary

Mary is a fifty-two-year-old college professor. She began therapy because of depression which was the result of her inability to get out of a destructive marriage situation. Also, she realized that her passivity, timidity, and general inability to change her marriage situation was typical of her entire lifestyle. Although she was a competent college professor, she was frequently passed over in being offered the preferred classes. She was convinced that she did not occupy the position of status in her department that, given her years of service, would have been appropriate.

She had no recollection of her natural parents. Her father had deserted her mother before Mary was born, and her mother had been killed in an automobile accident when Mary was two years old. She was then raised by her aunt and uncle. Her uncle was warm and loving, but her aunt was a severe and critical woman, and Mary had always felt rejected by her. Her uncle, of whom she was very fond, had died just before she left for college. Mary was a shy child, a lonely adolescent, who felt uncomfortable dating. She did well in school and was an effective teacher. She married a colleague with whom she shared intellectual interests, but the marriage turned out to be disappointing. She miscarried several pregnancies and was never able to have a child. The man she had married turned out to be petty and demanding, seemingly impossible to please. Although Mary felt stifled in the relationship, she had stayed in the marriage because she was too timid to do otherwise.

The diagnostic issues were complex in evaluating Mary. Although she had been affected significantly by the early loss of her mother, the non-nurturance of her hypercritical aunt, and the later death of her uncle, her major difficulty had been in the area of establishing a gratifying and intimate love relationship. Her very high level of ego functioning led me to conclude that her main difficulties were neurotic ones, predisposed by certain earlier oral traumas. Early in the therapy, Mary came to see that she had chosen her husband, for whom she did not feel much affection, because she had feared choosing someone she really loved, thus taking the risk of another great loss. She was also able to become aware of the warmth she had felt for her uncle, her jealousy of her aunt's relationship with her uncle, and her anger at her mother for having "left" her. At one point in the therapy, when I was about to leave for several weeks to attend a meditation retreat, Mary asked where I was going. Although this would be considered blurring a set boundary in terms of strict analytic technique, I told her. My decision to tell her where I would be was based, in part, on my knowing how frightening it was to her to have a "loved one" disappear. In addition, it seemed a good opportunity to introduce a transpersonal view.

While I was away on my meditation retreat, Mary read several books on Buddhist meditation that I had suggested. Since her academic field was literature and she was familiar with the works of Hesse and Kazantzakis, she had some intellectual understanding of Buddhist philosophy; however, she had not been aware of Buddhist meditation practice and had never considered meditation practice in any form for herself. Although her upbringing had been nominally Christian, Mary had no formal religious background. As an adult she had considered herself a scholar and an academic and had taken some pride in holding herself aloof from "irrational" religious practice. I feel sure that her primary motivation in considering Vipassana practice was that she knew I was committed to the practice and she admired me. Also, since no espousal of a belief system is necessary to begin meditation practice, it did not challenge her agnostic point of view. This particular fact about Vipassana practice, the fact that it has virtually no "religious" paraphernalia or rituals, has made it accessible to many of my patients who would otherwise have refused to consider a spiritual practice.

In the following year, Mary attended two ten-day meditation retreats. Over the course of both retreats she became aware, during meditation, of recollections of her mother and memories of the feelings of loss she had had at the time of her mother's death. During these experiences she was profoundly shaken. I want to emphasize the apparent power of this meditative approach to open up even pre-verbal areas of cognition. What Mary recovered were not memories of events, but rather feeling memories without cognitive thoughts attached to them. Since Mary was only two years old when her mother died and did not have any substantive memories of her early years, we supposed that her meditative experience had actually unearthed feelings from this early, preverbal period. In my experience, it has been rare to discover such depth feeling memories so vividly in so short a time using traditional psychotherapeutic approaches. When Mary resumed therapy after her retreat experience, she was able to use the material that had emerged in this deeply concentrated state to work with in therapy.

As therapy progressed, memories and feelings that had surfaced during the meditation retreat continued to emerge. Mary was able to see how her unwillingness to leave her husband and her general timidity were reflections of an early fear of being left alone or abandoned. She realized that her reluctance to seek out and enter into an intimate and gratifying relationship was based on her fear of loss, stemming from her experiences of losing her mother and her uncle. Her fears of her aggressive aunt, whose relationship she had envied, had kept her from assertively seeking to meet her own needs. As these issues became resolved, Mary's depression lifted, and she was able to terminate therapy.

Ultimately, she did leave her husband and in her follow-up contacts with me, her gains in therapy seemed to have been consolidated. Her work continues to go well, and she has begun a new relationship that seems quite gratifying. Her depression seems completely gone. She has continued her meditation practice.

My experience with Mary reaffirms for me the way in which Vipassana meditation practice may specifically facilitate depth psychotherapy. That is, in addition to the restorative and nurturing aspects of spending quiet time in a supportive community, the structure of the meditation itself seems to allow for the emergence of deeply repressed memories. Perhaps this is partly a reflection of the fact that as the mind becomes concentrated and calm, the contents of the mind are more clearly available for "viewing." I think it is also partly a reflection of the fact that the stimulus deprivation involved in meditation practice causes a breakdown of the ego defenses. In any event, when these early and profound memories do arise, especially in individuals whose ego structure is secure and steady enough to withstand, work through, and integrate these memories, Vipassana practice has proven to be a valuable adjunct to psychotherapy.

Case Study: Paul

In my psychotherapy work with Paul, I introduced no transpersonal issues or practices at all, since he had already been doing spiritual practice for many years. Indeed, the very symptom that brought this man into therapy was his feeling of discontent about his progress in his meditation practice. Paul was twenty-five years old and had been seriously practicing Zen meditation for four years when he came to see me. He was reasonably successful in his work as a computer engineer. He sought treatment because he felt his painful memories and feelings about his past were intruding into his meditation and hampering him from making any "spiritual" progress. He was also aware that, although he had had several gratifying relationships with women, he had always kept them on a superficial level. He recognized that every time a relationship progressed to a level of commitment, he managed, usually unconsciously, to undermine it. Also, even though he was competent in his job, he avoided taking the initiative in various work projects. Being successful at work projects might mean that he would be given a promotion, and he was aware that he was uncomfortable and anxious about being successful.

Paul had been raised by a very loving and supportive mother. His father, however, had been a cruel and vengeful man who frequently had beaten him. When I evaluated Paul, he seemed to me to show no evidence of any significant ego defect. I felt his conflict was an oedipal neurosis. I worked with him with traditional psychotherapy for two years. As painful and frightening material emerged and was worked through in the therapy, he found he had less experience of the same painful thoughts and feelings arising during meditation. Paul also had less anxiety about such thoughts and feelings emerging, even when meditating. He discovered he could be more assertive in his work without being anxious about "success." Likewise, he saw that his backing away in personal relationships was a way of avoiding the anxiety he felt about being successful.

He also realized that his sense of not making any progress in his meditative practice was a reflection of his psychological difficulties. In other words, Paul's anxiety about success included successful progress in his spiritual quest, which had been equated by him to an oedipal victory. He had needed to "fail" in his spiritual practice as a way of avoiding anxiety. As therapy progressed and oedipal issues continued to be worked through, he discovered he felt new vigor and enthusiasm in his meditation practice.

I have specifically included Paul's experience along with the previous three summaries of work with neurotic individuals because, although his presenting symptom had to do with the transpersonal issue of difficulty in his meditation practice, I felt that his problems were essentially neurotic. Also, because his problem was really a classical oedipal neurosis with no evidence of significant pre-neurotic fixations, he responded very successfully to traditional interpretive psychotherapy. Because he already had a spiritual practice and a spiritual belief system, there was no reason for me to introduce my own. I was, however, aware of how Paul's years of meditation practice had prepared him to be a good patient for this type of psychotherapy. He had a very keen sense of observing awareness, he had the patience to endure periods of emotional distress, and he had a healthy baseline of calm which he generally maintained. His years of practice had developed these uncommonly mature aspects in a still relatively young man.

Chapter 8

The Transpersonal Treatment of
Existential Problems

EXPLANATIONS OF PSYCHOLOGICAL DISTRESS at the existential level of psychosexual development differ from those of pre-neurotic or neurotic illness. In individuals with neurotic or pre-neurotic illness, it is possible to explain distress in terms of some developmental injury to psychological growth. Although we are psychologically sophisticated enough to realize that no one grows up without some emotional struggles, it is possible to imagine that, given a good genetic underpinning, a nurturing family, and good luck, people can grow up with healthy ego structures and no significant neurotic conflict.

My belief is that it is unlikely, even given optimum psychological health, for mature adults to pass through life without some consideration of the existential dilemma that life itself presents. It seems to me a fundamental part of human psychological experience to consider the temporality of life, the meaning of death, the question of purpose in life, and the possible broader significance of our experiences beyond that which we recognize and understand in our daily lives. Transpersonal psychology takes as a fundamental truth the notion that there is in all of us a basic inclination toward transcendence of our own personal egos in the direction of a broader connection with human consciousness as a whole.

I think it is rare that people seek out psychotherapists when their primary symptom is "existential angst." In my own professional experience it has usually been the case that patients present themselves with pressing interpersonal problems often indicated by painful and/or frightening psychological and physical symptoms. Usually these symptoms relate to difficulties in development from infancy through adolescence that have resulted in an impaired ego structure or poor ability to form gratifying interpersonal relationships. Also, it has often been my experience that, as individuals in therapy heal ego defects or resolve intrapsychic conflicts, they spontaneously begin to contemplate existential issues.

Sometimes people do come for therapy with existential issues as their main source of distress. This presents a particular dilemma for the therapist: their concerns either genuinely reflect a mature developmental level or may be an attempt to avoid dealing with conflict at a lower level of psychosexual development. For instance, I feel it would be a normal and appropriate reflection of psychological development for an individual with a well-consolidated ego, who is comfortable with interpersonal relationships and engaged in some meaningful work, to discover that he or she has feelings of emptiness or incompleteness. A sophisticated psychotherapist or a competent spiritual teacher might recognize this as an normal phase of ego development. Quite similar presenting symptoms of emptiness, meaninglessness, or yearning for transcendence in an individual with primitive ego development might well represent something quite different. It may be a defense against the anxiety that individuals feel in continuing to struggle, with fragile ego equipment, with the everyday problems of life, work, and personal relationships. A skilled therapist needs to take an accurate developmental history and listen very carefully to the dynamics of an individual's entire life situation to be able to make a good differential diagnosis in these kinds of cases.

The same diagnostic acuity is needed when patients present themselves in therapy with "transpersonal" physical symptoms. There is an ample catalogue of non-ordinary physical sensations and perceptions that arise in people who have undertaken meditation practice. Particularly frightening sensations and perceptions include a sense of being dissociated from one's body, variations in heaviness or lightness of the body, or even a sense of the body's disappearing. Although these experiences initially may be frightening, in a well-balanced and psychologically mature meditator, they do not necessarily present a problem, but these very same non-normal sensations and perceptions in a psychologically impaired individual are often symptomatic of severe emotional illness. "Transpersonal" body symptoms, therefore, need to be studied with the same careful diagnostic skill as the "transpersonal" psychological symptoms mentioned above.

The first three case summaries presented in this chapter have certain elements in common. In all three cases, a major presenting complaint was a dissatisfaction with life. In one instance, this dissatisfaction with life had become apparent upon the patient's retirement from active professional work. For another person, dissatisfaction arose when the breakup of her marriage seemed inevitable. In the third instance, the disappointment in life and despair over lack of meaning was coincident with the person's arrival at what should probably have been the high point of his professional career.

There is another point of similarity between the individuals in the first three case summaries. I decided to think of all of them as being, diagnostically, at the existential level of psychosexual development. I was aware, as I did so, that each of them had had some amount of psychological fixation at an earlier stage of development. There were, indeed, some indications of mildly maladaptive character styles present. I surmised from the fact that none of them had made gratifying intimate relationships that there were probably unresolved areas of oedipal conflict. However, none of these areas of fixation or conflict seemed substantial. I mention this point particularly for two reasons. First of all, it led me to concentrate on transpersonal issues with each of them and to weight the therapy in that direction, where I thought it would be most helpful. Also, although I did some interpretive work to help with areas of character style or neurotic conflict that were most obvious, that aspect of the therapy was minimal. All three individuals did well in therapy in a relatively short period of time, validating for me that this was the proper therapeutic approach. I include the fourth vignette, that of Marian, because her psychological and spiritual work continued to augment each other over some years in a way that clearly demonstrates their relevance to each other.

————————————— *Case Study: Nancy* —————————————

Nancy was a sixty-five-year-old, recently retired social worker when she sought therapy for her depression. Although she reported having been mildly depressed at various times during her life, her depression had worsened after her retirement. Her job had been her main source of gratification for several years. Her husband, a responsible but emotionally cool man, had died several years previously. She had been involved in two brief extramarital love affairs during her long marriage and, although both men had been willing to marry her, she had elected to remain in her marriage.

Nancy had three children, now living in distant cities, who were married with children of their own. While she was pleased that their lives were going well, she felt somewhat estranged from them. She felt disappointed that her life had turned out to be less fulfilling than she had hoped it would be. When I evaluated Nancy, I did not see any major problem in either pre-oedipal or oedipal areas. She seemed to me to have a somewhat harsh and self-critical character style which I felt represented an anal character structure. Although Nancy described her mother as a loving woman, she also said that she was a "super cleaner," quite meticulous, and was constantly putting pressure on Nancy to continually do better. When Nancy produced exam papers with a grade of 95, her mother would gently chide her about why she wasn't able to get the last five points. Nancy's father greatly favored her over her four-years-younger sister. When she was four years old, Nancy almost drowned, and her father literally saved her life.

I felt her inability to make a more satisfactory marriage or leave her basically unsatisfying situation had possibly been a reflection of some unresolved oedipal conflict. Her father had been a gentle man who took Nancy on private walks where they would share long conversations. Nancy recalled that she would often provoke disputes with her mother, which would result in her father taking sides. She reported that he normally supported her. However, neither her character style nor possible neurosis had seriously impaired her ability to live her life generally free from symptoms.

Although there certainly were some clearly oedipal issues in the material Nancy presented, they did not seem significant enough to be the cause of her current distress. I thought her situation seemed more to be one of tension around existential issues, rising out of a lack of feeling purpose in life. I surmised that these issues had surfaced at this point because of her recent retirement from professional work. Retirement, by its very nature, emphasizes the fact of the temporality of all life experience and the onset of old age. Therapy was generally of a supportive and instructive nature. Nancy was able to reconstruct and understand how her hypercritical view of herself was a reflection of how she had perceived her mother's view of her. She was also able to see how this critical style contributed to her depression. Discussions about purpose in life and the search for meaning were a major aspect of our work together. On my recommendation, she read Ken Wilber's *No Boundary*. Because she had been a social worker and was relatively psychologically sophisticated, she easily understood and appreciated this book. With my encouragement she attended several Vipassana meditation retreats.

Because Nancy had a relatively healthy ego structure, she was able to tolerate the sensory deprivation of the meditation retreat very well. However, she experienced many periods of tearfulness and intense depression. At those times, she felt overwhelmed with sadness, but was able to stay with those feelings until they began to pass. The experience of seeing these states pass spontaneously was very reassuring to her, making her depression seem less solid and formidable and, therefore, less frightening. When depressing feelings or memories arose, she was able to experience them without reacting to them with fear.

The retreat situation itself was also therapeutic for Nancy. She enjoyed a considerable sense of emotional support from being in the company of people with whom she felt she had a bond. The idea that she'd become involved with a group of people who were working toward a common goal partially answered her need to feel more meaning in her life. Since it is basic to Buddhism (and sacred tradition in general) that there is a wider perspective and larger goal than our generally narrow view of life and its goals, she was able to view her disappointments in this life as not as enormous as they had seemed.

I felt that Nancy's meditation practice was also responsible for a reduction of the harshness of her superego. She began to notice, both on meditation retreats and in her practice at home, that she experienced a sense of a dispassionate observing awareness that stood apart from the ups and downs of her daily experiences and observed her critical style, as well as her despair about it, with a certain amount of balance. With some effort, Nancy was finally able to accept her judgmental thoughts, oppressive and annoying as they were, as just part of the passing flow of events. To her great relief, she discovered that this brought about a reduction in her hypercritical style. She was later able to expand this insight to the realization that benign, balanced awareness of experience in general facilitates the "letting go" of all mind states. This was particularly significant to Nancy, since the presence of negative mind states such as disappointment, disillusion, and resignation had been a large part of her mental experience for many years and probably had been the underpinning of her mildly depressed state all of her life.

She was in therapy with me on a once-a-week basis for about a year. At the end of that time, her depression had virtually disappeared, and she had sufficient enthusiasm and vitality to plan an extended trip to visit relatives and old friends.

In the years since the termination of her therapy, Nancy has been in touch with me from time to time to let me know her progress. Her depression has not recurred. Although she has not continued to attend meditation retreats, she sets aside some period of time each day for quiet meditation at home. Also, she continues to read and take courses in the area of transpersonal psychology and philosophy.

In contrast to the preceding case summary of a woman whose "existential crisis" came at a predictable time of life—that of her retirement from active professional work—this next case summary is of therapy with a woman whose similar symptoms of depression and lack of purpose emerged in her early thirties. The traumatic event that seemed to precipitate her symptoms of depression and despair was the failure of her marriage.

Case Study: Kathryn

Kathryn was thirty-three years old when she sought treatment. She was very depressed about her failing marriage. Her husband was a man who had found it difficult to commit himself to a single relationship and had continued relationships with women outside the marriage. Kathryn, who had originally felt affection for her husband and who very much loved her two young children, was reluctant to divorce. She reacted to her husband's behavior by pouting, being extremely negative, and maintaining long periods of angry silence. Her behavior further alienated her husband, and their relationship continued to deteriorate.

Kathryn's mother had been a strict, angry woman. In large measure, Kathryn had identified with this aspect of her mother. Other than this characterological problem, however, she seemed to me psychologically quite healthy. She had been comfortable in her relationship with her father and enjoyed and valued relationships with men. Her sexual functioning was unimpaired. She had trained as an occupational therapist and had worked effectively before the births of her children.

When Kathryn first came into therapy, she was disappointed about the efforts she had put into her marriage, especially now that it seemed headed for divorce. She appeared disillusioned with life in general and had a vague uneasiness about how she would spend the rest of her life. I felt that her general level of psychological development was quite mature, and that her existential questions about the meaning of life were being particularly heightened because of the stress of her husband's behavior and the possible breakup of the marriage.

In working therapeutically with Kathryn, I used both a traditional interpretive approach, as a way of working with her character style, and a transpersonal approach, to help her with her depression. She quickly recreated, within the transference, the same relationship with me that she had had with her mother. That is, she imagined me to be critical of and angry with her, and she responded by pouting and being stubbornly silent. I was able to point out to Kathryn that she was relating to me as if I were her mother. While I could empathize with this angry style of response as a way of coping with her mother, I could also help her see that this same habitual silent response had been maladaptive in her adult life. Kathryn was increasingly able to soften this style, and she became quite pleasant and warm. She decided to divorce her husband and was able to handle his leaving with reasonable grace. As her style became more warm and relaxed, her relationships with her children became more spontaneous and gratifying. She resumed her work as an occupational therapist and found that to be rewarding.

Transpersonal issues came up naturally in the course of my therapy with Kathryn because her family was Japanese and she had been raised, at least nominally, as a Buddhist. She had rejected religion altogether as part of an adolescent rebellion phase. At some point in the therapy, I suggested that she read Joseph Goldstein's *The Experience of Insight*, an introduction to basic Buddhist concepts. The concept of attachment as a cause of suffering was very valuable for her. She would talk about how it was her attachment to having her husband stay with her (even though the marriage was ungratifying) that caused her pain. Kathryn realized she was attached to the self-image of a woman who could succeed in her marriage.

As she was more and more able to talk about the pain that came from her attachments, she was progressively able to let go of them.

In traditional terms, it might be speculated that Kathryn changed her ego ideal structure to a new ego ideal of someone with a spiritual approach who could overcome attachment. Whether a genuine overcoming of attachment took place or just a change of ego ideals seems to me irrelevant. A four-year follow-up after the termination of treatment showed that Kathryn had continued to consolidate her therapeutic gains. Her children were doing well, and she continued to be successful in her work. She had recently remarried, and that marriage seemed gratifying.

Case Study: John

Although I saw John and Marie together in joint therapy sessions, it was John who initially sought therapy on his own behalf. At that time he was forty-five years old and very successful in his work as an investment broker. His marriage, however, was at a crisis point. His wife was considering divorce, and their teenage son was showing symptoms of stress from the situation. Although John always seemed congenial to me in our initial contacts, he told me that his wife found him to be stubborn and rigid. He acknowledged that he knew it was thoughtless of him to make teasing remarks to his wife and son, and that they sometimes saw him as being cruel or hurtful.

John described Marie as rather cool, uncomfortable in showing affection. He said he sometimes felt jealous that she seemed to be able to express much more warmth and affection toward their son than she could toward him. As John described his background to me, I noted he had a very passive father and an aggressive, angry, domineering mother. John himself suggested that he recognized his mother's aggressive mocking style in the way that he related to his own son. In evaluating

John, I felt that although he had a rigid and aggressive character style, he did not have major neurotic or pre-neurotic pathology. His sexual functioning was unimpaired. His health was good. His work was successful and satisfying. He generally functioned without anxiety, although he was genuinely distressed about his marriage problem.

John's primary concern was with his marriage, which he valued and wanted to preserve. He expressed sadness about how his marriage situation seemed to be affecting his son. In addition to these concerns, he expressed a vague uneasiness about being at the midpoint of his life, at the height of his career, and not being "sure of what it is all about." He felt disillusioned about "having tried very hard" in his life and finding that it was not working out the way he had hoped it would.

I felt John's expression of existential concerns (his questions about meaning in life and disillusion with life's possibilities) was an appropriate and predictable response given his age, his high level of ego integration, and the considerable stress the family conflict had placed on him. I thought he was fundamentally a psychologically healthy man facing midlife issues—which necessarily bring up questions of meaning and purpose in life—with the additional burden of his relationship failure. In the course of my seeing John, I suggested that he read *No Boundary*, by Ken Wilber. He was particularly interested in Wilber's developmental schema, which posits that existential concerns are a normal and even desirable developmental phase. He was reassured by the notion that it is possible to have one's life in order, to be a "success," and still feel a sense of inner incompleteness. This validated his own persistent sense of disappointment in life and gave him some cause to believe that there was a way to work on these feelings.

John had sought therapy for himself, but since his main stressor was his failing marriage, I decided it would be more effective to work with John and his wife Marie in joint therapy sessions. I did some interpretive work with both of them, pointing out how some of their current styles of relating to each other reenacted the relationships they had had with their parents. My primary effort, however, was teaching them a more skillful, less aggressive way of relating to each other.

As they, by imitation or identification, became more gentle with each other, the general tension level in their marriage decreased, and they experienced more pleasure in their relationship.

Marie's background was more complex than her husband's, and I felt her level of neurotic conflict to be substantial. However, Marie was not as motivated to seek therapy as her husband was. Even if she had been, resolution of neurotic conflict generally takes some time. I felt that their marriage was at a stage of acute crisis, and that if it didn't improve immediately, they would divorce. I decided an approach that emphasized communication skills would be much more appropriate than long-term, intensive, interpretive therapy, which would add more stress to an already critical situation.

I had the opportunity to introduce the idea of studying *A Course in Miracles* to John and Marie after the therapy had proceeded for some months and the acute level of tension had passed. Although John had enjoyed reading psychological and philosophical literature, both he and his wife had negative feelings about religion and spiritual practice. They agreed, however, to read *A Course in Miracles*. I think their decision to do so was largely motivated by the positive feelings that they had about me, since I had been instrumental in helping them save their relationship.

Both John and Marie found that the emphasis *A Course in Miracles* places on forgiveness was what was most helpful to them. They both read the *Course* every day and practiced the daily meditations. Marie began to attend an *A Course in Miracles* study group once a week. Both of them found that by resolutely focusing on forgiveness they were able to attenuate their basically aggressive character styles. As both changed, the marriage continued to improve; as more warmth was generated in their relationship, they were less troubled by angry feelings and did not need to struggle so hard to keep these feelings in check.

After eighteen months of once-a-week sessions, I agreed with John and Marie that it was appropriate to terminate therapy. Their marriage crisis had resolved, their relationship was warmer than it had been at any time during their seventeen years of marriage, and their son seemed to be doing well. John particularly noted that his relationship with his son was much more warm and spontaneous than it had ever been.

Although the therapy did not have as a focus Marie's distrust of men, it did eventually emerge as John began to be kinder to her. Whereas in the past he would bully her verbally, he now was more empathic and kinder. To her surprise, this frightened Marie, because she no longer had a reason to be distant from him. She was able to see and admit then that she had often provoked him to be mean to her so that her distancing herself from him would be "understandable." At times when she used a more passive distancing maneuver, she saw how she was identifying with her weak and passive mother's style of relating to her father. Many of Marie's neurotic issues emerged with little or no effort, due solely to improved communication skills.

John was also able to recognize that part of his earlier feelings of despair and disillusion with life, which had seemed like transpersonal or existential issues, had been directly related to his (then) failing marriage. Now that his relationship had become more gratifying, issues of life and death and meaning and purpose seemed less pressing. He recognized them as issues of importance, which he wanted to work on further, so he continued to use *A Course in Miracles* as a way of meeting this need.

The final case summary is of work I did with a woman whom I first met fifteen years ago. At that time, Marian's symptoms were primarily neurotic, and I treated her with classical psychoanalytic therapy. Six years after what we both considered to be a successful completion of her therapy, I again worked with her in therapy for a few months. Her symptoms at that point seemed existential, very much like a midlife crisis, and the therapy was largely supportive and instructive. At my suggestion, she began Vipassana meditation. When I saw her most recently, her presenting symptoms sounded, on face value, much more ominous than any of her previous symptoms. She had episodes of depersonalization, periods of confusion, and other signs that ordinarily would be symptomatic of severe psychological illness. Because I had known her a long time, knew her to be relatively healthy, and knew that she had been doing intense meditation practice, I recognized these symptoms as predictable sequelae of meditation practice. I was able to reassure her about her fears and refer her back to meditation teachers.

Case Study: Marian

Marian is a forty-five-year-old high school language teacher who is married and the mother of three teenage sons. She first came to see me when she was twenty-eight years old, just after the birth of her third son. At that time she had symptoms of a classical hysterical neurosis, with some additional symptoms, particularly food phobias, that suggested some oral fixations. A particularly uncomfortable symptom for her was persistent hypochondriacal fear. Marian's mother, to whom she had been very close, had died of chronic liver disease when Marian was seventeen years old. Her father, an insurance salesman, was felt by Marian to have preferred her brother, who was two years her senior.

I treated Marian with classic psychoanalytic therapy three times a week for three years, until her symptoms had almost completely disappeared. Her food phobias seemed to be neurotic in nature, and as oedipal material was resolved, her eating problems lessened. Because her mother had been ill so often, much of the "feeding" of Marian had been done by her father. When she was four and five years old, it was frequently her father who organized her breakfast before he went to work in the morning and prepared her dinner when he returned home in the evening. This was their "special" time together and, clearly, Marian had eroticized this feeding experience.

During this time when she was generally anxiety-free, she continued to have what she herself recognized to be a hyperconcern about illness, and she resigned herself to having this as a character style that was part of identification with an ailing mother. She took up running, probably initially as a counter-phobic maneuver, and became a long-distance runner. Over the years, this helped her change her self-view from someone who was frail to someone who was healthy.

Six years after the termination of her therapy, Marian resumed therapy once a week for three months. Whereas she had been relatively symptom-free during the intervening years, she had begun to feel depressed following the death of her father one year previously. Her job, which in the past had given her considerable pleasure, had begun to seem routine. Her sons were no longer young children and did not require as much care as they had. The event that precipitated her coming to see me at that time was the death of a close friend, a woman her age whom she had known since childhood.

Work with Marian at this time was not interpretive, because I felt her depression was related to existential concerns. We talked of her worries about death and how the deaths of her father and friend had made her acutely aware of her own mortality. She felt that since she was no longer the mother of young children, part of her had "died." She was able to see how her preoccupation with death and with the need that life be meaningful drained her of energy, with the result that her otherwise interesting work now seemed routine.

After three months, Marian decided to terminate therapy because her depression had lifted. She reported that expressing the fears she had of death had made her feel more comfortable with them. She devised a new curriculum to use with her classes and felt that this was her way of creating something new, in lieu of a new baby. Marian was not interested in reading religious or mystical literature, since they seemed irrational to her; however, she did become interested in trying to learn to meditate when I explained that Vipassana meditation was a method of cultivating further self-awareness. She felt she needed to have an ongoing way of understanding herself without being in therapy. I think she also was interested in it because she knew it was a practice that I did, and she felt secure identifying with me.

A few years after this brief period of therapy, I received a long letter from Marian. She explained she had begun meditation practice by going on several weekend Vipassana retreats and had then attended two ten-day retreats in the course of the next year. She was writing because she felt I would be interested in knowing what her psychological experience had been in these intensive retreats. She described how she had been able, at least sometimes, to watch her thoughts and feelings from a distinctly observer stance. She explained how a single memory could trigger a succession of childhood memories, memories that had previously been very painful to her. In fact, she said, memories had come up that had never surfaced in her years of analysis. Without being explicit, Marian implied that she sometimes had had thoughts that were quite primitive, and she felt that if she had not experienced therapy, these thoughts would have been very frightening to her. She described in some detail the experience of having painful memories arise in consciousness and noticing that she was entirely comfortable and relaxed in watching these memories go by, "rather like an interested outsider." She seemed pleased to be able to report to me that she was well and particularly that she was "doing it on my own."

Marian returned recently, five years after she had last been in therapy with me. This time her symptoms were sudden, acute anxiety attacks and episodes of confusion in which things "seemed meaningless." She described these times as "losing the context within which things make sense so I don't know what's happening." She also reported instances of depersonalization. She said she could hear herself speaking but her voice seemed to be dissociated from her body. She sometimes had the feeling in the midst of a group that she was viewing herself interacting with other people, as if she were watching a movie. While she was continuing to function in her job and with her family, she felt a lot of anxiety even when her symptoms weren't present, worrying that they might recur at any moment.

In addition to previous symptoms, Marian said she had felt embarrassed to be "falling apart" and had, therefore, put off coming to see me. She said the meditation had been so helpful to her as a tool for personal awareness that she had hoped not to need any more therapy, and she had expected to continue to be symptom-free. She had pursued her meditation practice, meditating daily for an hour and attending at least two ten-day retreats every year.

Marian recalled that her current symptoms had started about six months previously when she had begun to experience some depersonalization episodes while teaching her classes. She would suddenly feel that although her body was still there and she could hear her voice talking, "she" was somehow not there. Also, she would begin to feel, in the midst of teaching something quite familiar to her, that she wasn't at all sure of what she was saying and that it did not seem to be important. She would occasionally have periods of confusion during ordinary activities such as shopping in a supermarket or talking to a friend. At other times, she would feel "empty, without any body sensations," and she developed the fear that she might disappear. It seemed that whenever any of these primary symptoms manifested, Marian would become very fearful, and the fear would trigger other symptoms such as dizziness, tachycardia, or simply high levels of anxiety.

I saw her only twice to evaluate the situation. Of primary significance to me was that, although she felt that her symptoms were bizarre and she had considerable anxiety about them, she maintained a very high level of functioning. In spite of her dissociative episodes, she taught all her classes, managed her household, was active in the nuclear disarmament movement, and, along with her husband, was running fifty miles a week and often competing in races on weekends. Her sons, two in high school and one in college, appeared to be functioning well.

I felt that Marian's symptoms were a reflection of some changes that were taking place as a result of her meditation practice, and I told her so. We talked about the possibility of viewing the situation more as a "restructuring of perception" than as "falling apart." She was aware that her symptoms were neither painful nor persistent. Her major distress came from worrying about the possible occurrence of symptoms rather than the symptoms themselves. She was relieved that I felt this did not require therapy and, indeed, that I thought that symptoms might be part of some desirable change. I referred her back to her meditation teachers for further guidance and advice with her meditation. I had a letter from Marian a month after we met, thanking me for the reassurance. Now that she was no longer alarmed about her symptoms, she said, they happened less frequently. She also reported that she had begun to find that some of the symptoms, particularly the sense of being able to watch her life as if it were a movie, were beginning to be enjoyable.

Two years later I had one more meeting with Marian. She wanted to discuss with me certain career changes she was planning, because she now saw me more in the role of a trusted friend than as her therapist. In that meeting, she seemed to me particularly relaxed and cheerful, and I commented on that. Marian agreed that she was much more relaxed than she had ever been. She explained it was a reflection both of her daily meditation practice and of what she felt were certain "insights" she had arrived at in intensive retreat practice. She reported her lifelong habit of worrying had largely disappeared, along with her hypochondria. Her recollection was that she had not been aware of these changes in any dramatic way, but rather, had become conscious of them by noticing their absence.

Chapter 9

Relationship Psychotherapy and Spiritual Traditions

RELATIONSHIP PSYCHOTHERAPY can justifiably be acknowledged as transpersonal psychotherapy from three perspectives. The first is that developing a successful relationship, one in which both partners enjoy a sense of contented attunement with each other, is a mini-version of our spiritual aspirations, our desire for a sense of non-alienation, of resting contented in our lives. The second is that my work with couples is based on my belief that our fundamental essence is loving and compassionate, which is more a spiritual perspective than the traditional, instinct-driven psychology view. Based on this belief, my therapeutic work with patients focuses on those obstacles, primarily experienced as fears, that block the expression of their natural essence. The third perspective is that I encourage patients to use tools such as meditation or prayer—whatever they feel comfortable with—from religious or spiritual paths to help attenuate fear and anger when they arise. I am convinced that in doing so they can more effectively develop the communication that will heal their relationships.

I believe that the essence of all spiritual paths is the experience of oneness with God or the All and the bringing of this experience back into the world. All spiritual practices strive to lessen the attachments to our individual egos that keep us from feeling at one with God or others. When we feel in love with or loving of others, we begin to lessen these ego attachments and move toward the experience of oneness. I no longer adhere to the traditional thera-peutic approach that sees human nature as dualistic: bad and good, black and white. My experience shows me that our core is loving. It is there, awaiting our recognition and nurturance. The image that comes to mind is that of the sun, which is always illuminated; we don't have to turn it on, we need only brush aside the clouds that at times obscure it. So it is with our hearts, which rest in lovingness. But that lovingness is difficult to see, to access, when fear systems take over. The goal of therapy thus becomes a process of uncovering the core of lovingness. Spiritual traditions have much to teach us about cultivating compassion and forgiveness, about tempering anger and learning acceptance.

My presentation of relationship work as spiritual practice sets a tone for the therapy that I do with couples. I do not think rela-tionship is a requirement for spiritual development—the monastic or celibate life, by choice or circumstance, includes the renunciation of sensual gratification, often a strong component for overcoming nar-cissism. But being in an intimate relationship, if that is one's path, does provide a different, ongoing, direct challenge to one's narcissism, since relational life requires constant modification of one's own desire in order to accommodate the needs of the partner, as well as provid-ing the support of feeling loved. The spiritual paths that I know all urge the development of compassion and kindness toward others as a way to experience interconnectedness, and the path of generosity and virtue is presented as the path to the fullest happiness.

In relationships, we are constantly called upon to express our own needs and desires in the context of what would be pleasing and helpful to our partners. Motivated by personal love and a desire to please, we can practice in a relationship a one-on-one version of what we hope to be able to feel in a wider sense toward *all* beings. When I work with couples, especially those who have an interest in religious or spiritual expression, I emphasize this aspect of our work together. I explain that the benefits of working out the problems in their relationship are multiple and expansive. Not only will they experience personal pleasure if they are successful, but they will, at the same time, discover ways to relate in a more loving and com-passionate way toward others.

My therapeutic work with couples focuses primarily on uncovering the fear and/or sadness that they experience in relationship to each other. As I believe that being loving is our basic nature, I think the ruptures that develop between people who have formerly loved each other reflect the ways in which the unconscious needs of each have come to be expressed in demands that alarm or disappoint the other. People often choose relationship partners to help replay a childhood trauma, hoping to use this new experience to heal the earlier wounding. Because these choices are unconscious, the tensions that develop when the new relationship does not heal those wounds are not easily identified.

It is my experience that people often fight about irrelevant issues because they don't know what the underlying need truly is. Generalized unhappiness manifests as anger, and people unskilled in the expression of anger often compound their difficulties either by fighting in vindictive or destructive ways, by withdrawing into a pouting, alienated distance, or by repressing (or *trying* to repress) the anger altogether. It is usually at this point—when any or all of these maladaptive attempts to deal with feelings of fear and sadness are activated—that couples come for therapy.

When I begin my work with a couple, I explain my conviction that the direct expression of anger is never helpful in resolving conflict. I make it clear that I do not advocate suppression of, or non-truthfulness about, feelings. I tell them that our work together will be directed toward their learning how to fully express their feelings in a way that can be metabolized constructively by their partner. The ideal, the goal, is for a patient to say things such as: "When you said that, I felt very angry, so probably I am frightened or sad. And now I need to figure out why I felt frightened, so I can tell you about it." In reality, however, I consider it a major advance when someone can replace his or her explosive anger with the comment, "I'm scared."

I use every possibility in our sessions to help couples discern the unconscious derivatives of their reactions and express them to each other. Frequently, it is these disclosures, these expressions of their deepest vulnerabilities, that bring couples closer together. They will often be able to start with very mildly threatening expressions of the fears beneath: "When you left that soiled sponge in the sink, you felt that I should clean it. I took that to mean that I, and my time, were not important. When I was growing up, my mother [or father] never treated me as if I was important." This is obviously just an example of a typical irritating situation that couples frequently find themselves in. It usually takes much work before that kind of comment can be elicited.

Ideally, over a period of time, as they see more clearly and trust more deeply, one person is able to say, "I am frightened that you, like my father, will never have a kind word for me . . . " or, "I am disappointed that you do not provide the unconditional love that my mother did not provide and that I thought you would . . . " The partner hearing the fear and/or sadness (perhaps for the first time) is often moved to compassionate response. Again, if the initial disclosure is simply, "I'm scared," this person is on the way. It will take a while for a patient to reach the level of understanding reflected in the remarks above, but it does happen, over time.

I use the technique of exploring with patients *any* anger that occurs at *any* time. "What are you afraid of?" My experience has taught me that beneath anger lies fear, and fear always, ultimately, comes down to the fear of death. In this, spiritual traditions can provide comfort: when one understands that there is no one there to die, when one really "gets it," fear of death diminishes. Discussing the fear of death can springboard into the areas of spiritual dimension, the "God spark" within us, and lead the patient to find ways, often "spiritual" ways, to cope with that anxiety.

One way in which I make it possible for people to admit their vulnerabilities and their fears is by explaining the varying levels of response we have, based on different levels of brain physiology. Harville Hendrix, in *Keeping the Love You Find* (306), presents the idea that our most instinctive response to a threat is based in the amygdala, a part of the midbrain, and in the "old brain," or "reptilian brain." Perceptions on this level are processed in terms of threatening or non-threatening, with no modifying nuance. Our reptilian or most primitive brain sees things in terms of an automatic reflexive "eat or be eaten" view. The amygdala is part of the limbic system in the midbrain and is found in lower mammals as well as in man. It seems to be a very important part of our survival brain, and is necessary to experience fear, which then sets up the fight or flight mechanism. Thus, anger and rage also seem to be involved with the midbrain or limbic system. The response to a threat perceived on this level cannot be other than to attack or flee.

Brain impulses are said to travel from this portion of the brain at least twice as fast as they do to and from the "newer" cerebral cortex, the more mature part of the brain which, literally, can think things over and make alternative choices. In addition, nerve impulses from our five senses travel directly to the amygdala without having to travel first to the neocortex, which is our highest brain and most developed in man. We can think of our reptilian and midbrain to be the reflexive and quick action regulators that help us survive danger. Evolution has wisely prepared us for survival by not requiring our neocortex to be operational in an emergency where our life is threatened. A bit later, the neocortex can come into operation with planning, reflecting, or even canceling plans of the reptilian and midbrains. In a situation that is perceived as a threat, the reptilian and midbrain may swiftly "kidnap" or take over the rest of the brain and counterattack.

In the lower animal world, this is an adaptive survival mechanism. In a love relationship, however, the survival brain (reptilian and midbrain) response is usually destructive. Here is a vignette that demonstrates this point.

Case Study: Joelle and Martha

Joelle and Martha had been a lesbian couple for a very long time. Martha experienced physical rejection in her first year of life and used to scream loudly for food. As a young woman, she felt more comfortable when the refrigerator and freezer were well stocked. Her more primitive anxieties most often showed up in her style of approach to life, rather than in any discernible psychopathology. Since Joelle was less worried and more relaxed in these areas, they didn't have too many conflicts.

Together, they had done a good deal of psychological work on their relationship and knew where most of their "buttons" were. They decided to remodel a guest cottage on their property, and Martha wanted to make sure that they included a significantly large refrigerator and stove for the storage and preparation of food. Joelle, however, insisted that the aesthetics of the small room would be impaired by oversized kitchen equipment. Martha experienced instant rage at Joelle for her insensitivity to her viewpoint and wishes. Because of our work together, Martha contained the rage with some facial grimaces and a mild pout, while she internally struggled to find out what so enraged/frightened her. As soon as she reminded herself of her lifelong anxiety about provisions, stocked larders, etc., the rage totally disappeared, and she was able to explain to Joelle what her feelings were and where they came from. Joelle had initially responded to Martha relatively slowly, a sign of new brain-cerebral cortex processing, and she herself was not feeling personally threatened. Martha had actually experienced Joelle's relatively mild negative comments about the proposed kitchen renovation as a death threat, since large, well-stocked larders represented survival to her, and she was aware that she had become enraged in a split second. As frequently happens in these types of episodes, Joelle later felt compassion for Martha. She sincerely and lovingly told her to renovate the cottage in whatever way made her most comfortable. Likewise, Martha, having moved from reptilian and midbrain type of response to her more reasonable cerebral neocortex-cognitive thinking response, was able to see the unreasonableness of her position and was much more comfortable now with Joelle's aesthetic viewpoint.

It has been my experience that Martha and Joelle's communication dilemma is typically the root of relationship difficulties. Since we very often pick partners who will unknowingly help replay our childhood traumas, the reptilian-midbrain fears of our childhood will be activated in our adult relationships. I also believe that the earlier in life one experiences psychological or physical trauma, the more strongly relationship conflict will be perceived as life-threatening, thereby activating our reptilian-midbrain system type of reflexive thinking and acting to "stay alive." Although the participants in a conflict believe they are disagreeing or arguing about a surface issue, the reptilian-midbrain reflex manifests as a way of "surviving." It is valuable for people to understand that the ways in which they respond and react are probably more directly related to experiences in the past than to the experience at hand.

Couples who have learned this are less likely to fight with each other, and each is more likely to use his or her partner as a support for healing. This becomes all the more obvious when we realize that our partner also has a survival (reptilian-midbrain) brain. Depending on what traumas they may have experienced, our aggressive or angry communications will cause them to go into fight or flight mode. When couples fight, more often than not the survival brain of each person is directing the communication, with lesser varying amounts (from nothing to some) of the communication being directed by the highest or neocortical brain. In fact, couples usually report later, when things are calmer, that they don't know what was so upsetting. From the vantage point of our neocortex, this makes sense, since so many of our survival techniques are not logically to be used in our relationship. Our fighting (verbally or physically) or fleeing (pouting, withdrawing, or leaving) are remnants of these earlier mechanisms and, I believe, never work in the best interest of the relationship. Even in a civilized world, we still need some of these survival mechanisms for emergency situations. But these mechanisms are frequently activated and "in charge" to a degree that is patently counterproductive in a relationship.

Our knowledge of post traumatic stress disorder (PTSD) gives us valuable clues in understanding some issues in relational difficulties. For example, a Vietnam veteran with PTSD might be walking down the street in a city in the United States and hear a car backfire. Before he can think in his neocortex, "There is no shelling going on here," he has hurled himself to the ground. That is the survival brain in action. If the earlier trauma was extremely threatening or stressful, *we would be incapable* of resisting the impulse to fight or flee. Fortunately for us, most relational problems are not of this severity. Though the fear recorded in the amygdala will never go away, over time the prefrontal cortex *can* suppress the amygdala's fear response. Here too, spiritual practices can help calm the mind and encourage the cortical response over the more primitive reaction. Dr. Joseph LeDoux, a neuroscientist at the Center for Neural Science at New York University, says that our early, midbrain emotional systems seem to be hard-wired. In therapy the patient can learn how to inhibit the action of the amygdala. The emotion will remain, but it will become less dominant.

LeDoux discovered how the amygdala takes control over the neocortex. The former's pathways are much more rapid, and action will often be taken on the amygdala's response before the neocortex, with its reasoning power, can consider the options and make a decision. Indeed, there is a neural shortcut to the amygdala that totally bypasses the neocortex.

Far from supporting the expression of anger, research (by Zillmann, Mallick, and McCandless) has shown that the expression of anger can prolong and intensify feelings while, at the same time, igniting angry feelings in the person to whom the anger is expressed. Angry reactions between two people are often messages from the amygdala of one brain to the amygdala of the other, with no neocortical activity.

I do not believe the expression of anger and rage by the reptilian-limbic system part of our brain can help the individual to grow, mature, and become more loving. Relationships heal *despite* the expression of anger and not because of it. The older survival brain tends not to *listen* to cognitive reasonableness, but rather reacts on the basis of direct *experience*. The reptilian-midbrain can begin to relax and become less reactive when it has the experience of safety and comfort over a relatively long period—a strength that becomes available in long-term, committed relationships.

Daniel Goleman's book *Emotional Intelligence* describes the astonishing research being done on the brain, on the amygdala's responses, and the implications of what is being discovered. It has been found that to experience empathy one must be tranquil and open. In couples therapy, therefore, what could be more conducive to promoting empathic responses than a technique of meditation from a spiritual tradition? Practicing meditation can lay the groundwork for understanding by calming the mind and opening the heart. When a couple fight, and the amygdala circuitry is involved, any possibility of sympathetic response has already been lost if the fear/anger evolutionary response is operational (for the organism to survive).

I involve couples in a therapeutic alliance with me as we begin therapy, by being supportive of their attempt to reconcile and expressing optimism about their ability to do so when that seems reasonable. I tell people that if they ever felt loving toward each other and excited about being together, the chances are that those feelings can be rehabilitated. I ask for their support in the therapeutic enterprise by requiring them to relinquish the direct expression of anger and try to express their anger in terms of feeling frightened or sad. I point out that if they cannot manage a non-aggressive presentation of their feelings outside of therapy, they should wait until our therapy session to discuss it. I explain that I understand that this will be difficult, as it means they are also relinquishing the tension relief that comes from an angry outburst. But I encourage them to work at it. I tell them that I believe that at some level the anger they feel is a remnant of an old response to something life-threatening, and that our work together will try to explore this derivative fully in order to heal it. I describe the reptilian-midbrain response, employing this image to encourage them to soothe each other's more primitive feelings. I assure them that, as loving support replaces aggressive fighting, the old survival brains will become less reactive, and the new brain will be able to assume more power. This will enable them to listen and evaluate current experience with cognitive, discriminating abilities that will then allow for making sounder choices.

Part of my therapeutic technique is to help people see directly that their anger is a reflection of a fear that is fundamentally experienced as life-threatening. Because I sometimes need to push people to examine their responses much more closely than they would otherwise, I must solicit their help in doing this. I will say, before following a line of reasoning, "Please go along with me as we follow this feeling, even if the line of questioning doesn't seem clear or reasonable to you." Usually, people agree and are surprised to find that a fear of death underlies their anger.

When the level of depression and/or rage in a patient is great, I have found that the judicious use of certain medications can transform a totally unworkable relationship into one that has a chance for rehabilitation. Some of the new antidepressants, specifically the SSRIs (Prozac, Zolof, Paxil, etc.) which act to increase our serotonin levels can, with *skilled* application, greatly facilitate the psychological healing of a relationship. I have seen a variety of positive results in patients, including noticeable calming of the hyperrage, a significant lowering of the level of anxiety, a decrease in the depth of depression, a lessening of sensitivity to criticism, and a diminution of perfectionism, which is often a problem in a relationship.

Anger, even at the level of rage, is frequently experienced with "righteous indignation," as if it made sense to be angry or as if the anger would help amend the situation. Here, patients of mine in couples therapy report that they have just had a terrible week.

Case Study: Tim and Sally

Tim had been complaining and finding fault with everything that Sally said or did. He felt justified because, he said, "My boss is talking about downsizing the company, and I may lose my job. So, I'm edgy, and Sally isn't supportive."

"Why would it bother you to lose your job?" I asked.

He seemed startled by the question, but responded, "I'm not sure where I can get another one."

"Why would that bother you?" Again, he seemed startled, as my questioning seemed naive.

"I'd have no money," he said. "My family would starve . . . My wife would leave me . . . No one would respect me . . . I would be embarrassed to tell my parents . . . If my parents and my wife don't love me, I'd be alone . . . "

"Why would it bother you to be alone?"

"I would die if I were alone."

Here we see uncovered the ancient fear of the small child who lives within the patient. Our adult, neocortical brain knows that we can drive to the supermarket to buy bread and milk and can survive quite well. Our child within us is closer to our survival brain's mode of thinking and tends to react from that place, leading to fight or flight mechanisms which for the moment can "kidnap" our adult, neocortical brain, whose logic might otherwise mitigate our response to a more appropriate one that would benefit the relationship. On occasion, this fear provides the patient with a springboard to move into the spiritual dimension, to offer spiritual ways to cope with the fear, and to deal with questions about meaning and survival of consciousness.

What is important, I believe, is not the specific fears that people express. What seems transformative in the relationship is the discovery that what was previously experienced as anger is actually an expression of fear. When people see this directly, they are motivated to reframe their angry communications in terms of the fears they represent. This level of communication most often elicits sympathy and compassion instead of rebuttal and retaliation.

Case Study: Ben and Wendy

Ben and Wendy were Zen Buddhist meditators who had met in Japan while on a spiritual pilgrimage. They shared many values, supported each other's spiritual aspirations, and were devoted to their young sons. Their marriage, however, seemed to be deteriorating under the strain of Wendy's habit of nagging and Ben's sullen withdrawal response. They sought therapy because they hoped they could regain the affection and warmth they had originally shared.

One day the therapy session began with Ben reporting he had become enraged at Wendy for leaving a pile of papers on the floor in a "messy" way. Following the style of questioning of "Why would it bother you that there was a mess on the floor," Ben recalled that when he was a child his mother had beaten him for leaving messes. He remembered the anxiety he had felt when she came into his room, lest the room not be tidy enough. Since he identified himself with his household, he needed it to be tidy at all times to avoid feeling anxious. Although his mother had died five years previously, any mess made him feel in danger of incurring her wrath. His thinking-level brain knew that it was just a pile of papers on the floor, but his instinctive response, originating from the older reptilian-midbrain, was alarmed about being beaten and unloved. As Wendy watched Ben's breakdown, she was moved by how she had, inadvertently, caused him to be frightened, and she reached out to comfort him. Such poignant moments occur frequently in this type of therapy and seem to be significantly healing.

Working with this couple and with some others, too, it is clear that it is not always necessary to access the fear of death by one partner in order to elicit empathy in the other partner. Often, just seeing the childhood fear of a significant parent is enough to evoke this empathy and compassion. I am convinced that if pushed further beyond the "fear of mother" situation that was tapped into, the fear of death by the very-young-child Ben would have been accessed.

The question can be legitimately asked: What would the reaction be from a person who had a very positive early ego development where there was not any major breach of the empathic and trusting bond? In almost every situation I have worked with, the fear of death was accessed behind the anger. Where I have not been able to elicit this, I am not sure whether or not it was due to a resistance to my approach—which to some is annoying or bothersome because the line of questioning seems so stupid (*and*, I believe, threatening).

I have observed through my therapy work with couples and with individuals that there is often a surprising difference in the pace of the work, which I've not seen discussed. When working with a couple, I find that as a rule they can access their problems more rapidly than people I see in individual therapy. A couple, practicing their transference distortions with each other day and night, come into a session together with their transferences already at a heightened pitch. In individual therapy, on the other hand, it tends to take a significantly longer time for events to occur to set off the transference responses that then lead to the healing work.

Furthermore, in couples' therapy, it seems to me that there are three patients: Patient A, Patient B, and Patient C (the relationship). This creates a distinctly different dynamic than that of individual therapy, and moreover I believe, this contributes to the reasons that couples' therapy often moves appreciably faster than one-on-one treatment, especially at the start.

I often reassure a couple by pointing out to them that traumas stemming from early childhood may take a very long time (ten, twenty, or thirty years) to heal in a generally safe and caring relationship. Usually, as we become less frightened we have more energy for, and are more open to, a spiritual pursuit. Unresolved psychological problems will often negatively distort the spiritual journey. A committed, caring relationship offers one of the most powerful tools I know of for psychological, as well as spiritual, healing.

Sometimes patients are not able to grasp at first the process of delving beneath their anger to find the fear. Their reluctance can stem from a variety of causes, and I have found that introducing them to forgiveness practice is often very valuable. In the major spiritual traditions, various techniques have been taught to work with anger. Forgiveness practice can pave the way for a couple to see each other not only more clearly but with compassion. And finding compassion for one's partner will certainly ease tensions and help free one to deal with the issues from a more peaceful place.

An important facet of the forgiveness practice, furthermore, is the discovery of *self-forgiveness*—an opening of one's heart to oneself. This discovery can be very important, and it can bring a new dimension of acceptance and love to a couple's process as they explore their anger together. It can even hasten their understanding that there are fears beneath the anger. Allowing themselves to have compassion for themselves (and each other) permits them to move *beyond* the anger.

How can a long-term, committed relationship help us advance along our spiritual path? All of the great spiritual traditions speak of how our attachments can stand in the way of spiritual advancement—attachments to our (small) ego, (small) self (as opposed to our higher Self), material needs and wants, bodily grati-fications, etc. We are all imperfect individuals with varying degrees of selfishness or unhealthy narcissism.

There is no way one can be in a long-term, committed rela-tionship without having to acknowledge and struggle with these issues. In short-term relationships, it is possible to hide these areas from view, but not in long-term relationships. I frequently tell couples that in their essence they are like two pure diamonds with varying amounts of psychological rough edges obscuring their brilliance. In a successful committed relationship, the couple needs to "skillfully" pol-ish the roughness covering the brilliance of their respective diamonds. To rub too abrasively on each other can damage the diamonds, and conversely, to not rub at all leaves us with our inner brilliance and potential not realized.

If there are children in the committed relationship, the "rub-bing" process, with the additional need to gratify the healthy requirements of child rearing, can be even faster, though often more dangerous and threatening. The reptilian-midbrain of the adult will, unfortunately all too often, stand in conflict with the child, leading the adult to damage the child, as we frequently see in child abuse. To optimally parent a child requires that there be a minimal amount of pathologic narcissism present in the parent.

Thich Nhat Hanh, a Buddhist monk, in *Touching Peace: Practicing the Art of Mindful Living,* says: "Interpersonal relation-ships are the key for success in . . . [spiritual] practice. Without an intimate deep relationship with at least one person, transformation is unlikely."(107) Here again, we see how what appears to be a more traditionally oriented psychotherapy of relationships is actually cre-ating an important prerequisite for a successful spiritual practice. In fact, the danger of not being able to experience real intimacy with at least one person is that no matter what spiritual gains are made, they will be expressed through pathologic narcissistic channels. This can be seen in spiritual communities where a leader uses fol-lowers in destructive ways.

Michael Washburn, in *Transpersonal Psychology in Psycho-analytic Perspective*, also affirms the importance of developing inti-mate relationships with another, or others, as a prerequisite for the development of spiritual wholeness. This development of intimacy is not usually achieved until midlife, when traditionally the final ascent along the path of spiritual transcendence begins. Washburn points out that the development of intimacy requires effective dualistic ego functions, i.e., seeing oneself as separate from others (usually during the first half of life), while the lessening of the dualism of the ego is then required in order to attain greater psychospiritual wholeness.

Sometimes I work with couples who have no particular interest in spiritual development. In those instances, the therapy can proceed on the basis of uncovering fears and sharing vulnerabilities and still be very helpful. My experience has been that the therapy is potentiated when couples do have a spiritual interest, and I support these interests whenever there is an opportunity. For example, the great spiritual traditions that I know all teach about the harmfulness of the direct expression of anger. As I begin to work with patients, in addition to sharing my own conviction that spontaneous outbursts of anger are not helpful, I might underline my conviction with a reference to a tradition that I think is meaningful to them.

Traditional Christian teachings present Jesus as the model *Source* of forgiveness in all situations. Also, the Christian-based *A Course in Miracles* teaches that we should never express anger toward others because we are, in that moment, unable to see clearly our interconnectedness with others. If we saw clearly, if we knew all of the dimensions of our feelings, we would see that our anger is fear-based, that the situation would be best handled by clear, mutual explanations of need and of the underlying fears, rather than by outrage.

Buddhist teachings present anger as one of the "defilements" that cloud the mind. Verse Two of *The Dhammapada* reads, "All things have the nature of mind. Mind is the chief and takes the lead. If the mind is polluted, whatever you do or say leads to suffering which will follow you as a cart trails a horse." Verse Five says, "Your enemies will never make peace in the face of hatred. It is the absence of hatred that leads to peace. This is an eternal truth." Verse Six says, "We are but guests visiting this world, though most of us do not know this. Those who see the real situation are not inclined to quarrel."

Specific practices from spiritual traditions can play a significant role in people's attempts to communicate skillfully with each
other. Those people who have a meditation or prayer practice often
find that periods of quiet reflection help them put whatever they
want to say into a perspective that can be more positively commu-
nicated to their partner. Meditators in all traditions, who practice
attentiveness to the sequence of thoughts and states that arise in
the mind, are often more easily able to recognize the perception-
thought-fear-anger sequence as it happens. Consequently, they are
often more capable of expressing the underlying core of fear that led
to angry feeling than are people without this training.

A specific practice from the Buddhist tradition is the cultivation of Right Speech, speech that is truthful *and* helpful. In the
Vinaya, the catalog of monk's rules as taught by the Buddha,
admonishing a person is permissible only after reflecting on
whether the admonition is timely, truthful, gentle, useful, and kind
(*Some Sayings of the Buddha*, 24). People quickly grasp that what
this means is that negative speech can be destructive and, therefore, calls for careful reflection.

Sometimes patients will object to my emphasis on meticu-
lously careful speech, suggesting that this leaves no room for
spontaneity. I believe emotionally mature couples (people who
normally do not come for therapy) are able to metabolize momen-
tary irritability between them without significant loss of close-
ness. These couples can be comfortable being spontaneous and
relaxed. However, where there is significant early psychological
trauma and/or a predisposition to hypersensitivity to criticism,
even small outbursts of anger can lead to fear and loss of trust on
a primitive level. I assure the people I see in therapy that emphasizing Right Speech is a useful tool with which to form a relationship based on trust. It will allow the couple someday to feel more
relaxed together, with spontaneity less of a threat to the stability
of the relationship.

Miriam and Irving illustrate that the "speech" in Right
Speech includes the many subtleties of body language, tone, and other
physical nuances.

──────── *Case Study: Miriam and Irving* ────────

Miriam, age thirty-five, and Irving, age thirty-nine, had been married eight years and worked together as psychotherapists. Both had had many years of individual psychotherapy before coming to see me, during which time they seemed to have resolved most of their significant neurotic conflicts.

Miriam came from an intact Jewish family. Her mother was the authority in the family—pushy and demanding. Her father was loving but weak and passive. Miriam's stubbornness and pushiness seemed to stem from her conflicts and identification with her mother. Irving, like her mother, frequently scowled and made a "bad face" at Miriam when he was upset.

Irving also came from a non-observant Jewish family which exhibited the reverse dynamics of Miriam's. His father, a Wall Street stockbroker, was harsh and hypercritical, while his mother allowed herself to be bullied by her husband. When his father got angry, he mostly held it in and fumed silently, with little doubt in anyone's mind about what he was feeling.

Miriam had unconsciously picked her "mother" to marry, as Irving had selected his "father." Each seemingly did this to heal those childhood wounds still remaining, i.e., they recreated the original trauma but now hoped to have it come out differently and be healed. Because they were both psychotherapists, they tried to use calm, sophisticated language to communicate. Miriam was making efforts to be different than her mother had been in her marriage, and Irving, who so frequently had been the butt of his father's anger, had been trying conscientiously to relate to Miriam in ways that differed from those his father had used. However, when Miriam and Irving did upset each other, they reverted to their earlier identification patterns. They had enough neocortical brain function to avoid open hostility: their telltale signals of anger would come with an eye movement, clenching jaw muscles, tightening neck muscles, a wave of the hand, or a glazed look on the face. As we probed under each of these "molehills," we found the "mountain" that, when pursued, most often led to an underlying fear that was being hidden in the moment.

Buddhist Vipassana (mindfulness) meditation can be used as a technique to train the mind to witness the arising of anger and not react impulsively and destructively to it. Such techniques can be seen as methods to train the mind to *avoid* being kidnapped by the reptilian and midbrain when the individual is frightened.

After one uncovers what lies beneath the anger, one's reaction to it can be changed. Forgiveness practices from spiritual traditions can hasten and enhance the awareness or even provide an alternate route to the awareness when traditional talking therapy does not seem to be providing the necessary clarity of mind.

Ken and Fran consulted me because their fifteen-year marriage was in danger of falling apart due to the rage attacks Ken had during arguments with Fran. He would lose his temper and throw things at her. The immediate precipitating event would often be Fran's emotional withdrawal or threats to leave the marriage.

Case Study: Ken and Fran

Ken was a forty-year-old art teacher at the local junior college, and Fran was a successful stockbroker in a brokerage firm. They had two daughters, ages ten and thirteen. Both Ken and Fran came from homes where they had experienced benign neglect and a sense of not being cared for.

In classic fashion, they seemed to have "picked" each other to replicate the feelings of aloneness that they had experienced in their early childhoods. I questioned Ken about the rages he experienced when Fran threatened to leave him. As we tried to access the fear behind the rage, Ken suddenly had trouble breathing, began gasping, and suddenly remembered that he had almost died of asphyxiation as a seven-year-old child, when he had pneumonia. His earlier condition had necessitated being rushed to the hospital emergency room. He had stopped breathing, and it had required emergency intubation and artificial respirators to revive him. Ken told me how he had had an out-of-body experience, during which time he watched the physicians working on him. He remembered that while in the out-of-body state his favorite grandmother, who had died a year before, came to him, saying that it was not his time to die yet and that he had much to learn in this life.

By now, in my office, Ken was breathing much more easily and could readily see how Fran's threatening to leave him activated his terror of being left alone—it had been during one of the periods of being left alone by his mother (who had gone out for the evening) that the asphyxiation event had occurred.

Further work with Ken along these lines was very helpful in alleviating the rage reactions to Fran. He would say somewhat lightheartedly, "I guess my problem is that I am afraid to let go [of life]."

I believe that our DNA is programmed for survival. Even an amoeba will try to survive by swimming away from a noxious substance. As long as we identify ourselves with our physical body, our DNA coding will fear extinction and try to survive. Many advanced spiritual beings have little attachment to their bodies—seeing themselves as more attached to their spiritual essence—and therefore have no fear of dying. As a result of this, I believe they seem more loving.

During our initial interviews, I found that Ken and Fran had a newly emerging interest in spiritual issues, although their main interest seemed to be in developing psychic powers.

Although *A Course in Miracles* was not a path devoted to the development of psychic powers, I suggested to them that it might be a route that could offer them some help. I chose the *Course* because Ken and Fran both had Christian backgrounds that were meaningful to them. Also, *A Course in Miracles* suggests that we are here to learn different lessons from each other on the path to becoming more loving, and I believed this concept would be helpful to them. I felt that since there was a great deal of loving and friendship still in the marriage, this approach would begin to give them an open area in which they could begin to look at the negative aspects of their relationship.

Because of their early traumas in their families of origin, both had fears of intimacy, lest they be retraumatized. They therefore used a narcissistic character style, which most often reflected in emotional withdrawal and "selfish" demandings from each other that were not fulfillable and served to keep intimacy at bay. Their study of *A Course in Miracles* began to give them the courage and positive attitude to help each other with the fears that lay behind their "selfish-looking" approaches to life. This new spark revitalized their enthusiasm to make the marriage work, even if it would take a long time to do so.

I gained a new understanding from my work with this couple. Because of Ken's near-death experience at the age of seven, he had no conscious fear of death and was even looking forward to it, as he saw it as an opportunity to be united with his beloved grandmother and many other friends who had since died. From this, I conclude that it is the survival brains (reptilian and midbrain limbic system) that are encoded with the fear of death or the drive for survival of our physical bodies. Our highest brain (neocortex) can transcend the fear of death with, for example, various spiritual practices. Some of us may have opportunities to explore the theoretical implications this has for working with rage and fear.

Karl came to me alone for individual therapy and then later brought his wife, Kathy, for couples' therapy. Their case illustrates a number of significant issues: 1) that psychological healing can be helped and potentiated with meditation and judicious use of medication, 2) that many individuals are resistant to the use of medications, some for the reasons in this case study (and others for reasons as outlined by Peter Kramer in *Listening to Prozac*), and 3) that certain medications can potentiate the meditative experience.

─────── *Case Study: Karl and Kathy* ───────

Karl initially came to see me for help with his failing marriage, although he did so reluctantly. He was in his mid-fifties, had a Masters degree in social work and had been working for twenty years at a clinic run by Catholic Social Services, where he worked primarily with new immigrants from Central and South America. His reluctance about therapy had several components. One was chagrin over what he characterized as his "inability to choose wisely." He felt that he should have had enough psychological sophistication to see that Kathy would replay the same dynamics that had led to the failure of his first two marriages. In addition, he had a serious interest in Buddhism and meditation (having decided to contact me after meeting me at a Vipassana retreat), as well as a continuing, dedicated practice as a Catholic. He felt that he "should" be able to use his spiritual practices to develop sufficient calm and resignation to accept his current situation without resentment. He hoped to convince himself of the spiritual merit of renouncing his own needs and desires, but it wasn't working. His final resistance was his general distrust of Western therapies and Western medicine. Presumably, my presence at the meditation retreat allowed him to contact me.

Karl had grown up in a large Catholic family in a midwestern city. He was the second child, first son, with seven younger siblings. Karl's father was a surgeon. The family was financially secure, but Karl recalled that his father was away from home working long hours, characterizing him as an "absent father." He told me that, apart from appearing with the family at Sunday Mass, his father was rarely at home.

He described his mother as seeming "perennially flustered" by her large family with its many demands, even though the family's finances allowed her to have extra household help. His mother had migraine headaches and periodically would need to retire to her bed for several days. Even as a young boy, Karl would try to care for his mother during her headache times, tiptoeing into her room, bringing her cool compresses for her head. He told me that he knew as a child that he was her favorite and that he both secretly enjoyed that status and also felt a little guilty about it. He remembered feeling especially good when she would need something—her reading glasses, an extra sweater—and look immediately to him to fetch it for her. He enjoyed the "special smile" she would give him as a reward.

As Karl reached adolescence, his father became a significant factor in his life. According to Karl, his father became stricter, more heavy-handed in his discipline. As a teenager in the early sixties, Karl participated in the prevailing rebellion against "everyone over thirty." It was a strong factor in Karl's choice to drop out of the local university after one year. (Because it was near his house, he had lived at home as a freshman and felt he needed to get away.)

After Karl spent several years travelling, he settled in San Francisco, where he worked at a Catholic home for delinquent and/or orphan boys, and there became active as a counselor for men who, like himself, wanted conscientious objector status from the draft. As a devout Catholic, a vegetarian, and a pacifist, he achieved that status for himself.

Karl met his first wife while travelling, and she was his first serious relationship outside the scrutiny of his family home. She had been drawn to his solicitous, caretaking nature, and he used his capacity to anticipate the whims of needy women—which he had learned in relationship to his mother— to charm her. They married after a brief courtship, since his religious upbringing made him uncomfortable about sexual freedom. He was soon feeling neglected and disappointed. Whereas his caregiving of his mother had resulted in her treating him as "most favored," his wife treated him with disinterest. The more depressed he became, the more demanding she became. Their arguments became heated, and she left him, quite suddenly, for another man. Because she disappeared, he was able to have the marriage annulled.

Depressed and angry, Karl returned to college, finished his undergraduate degree, and entered social work school. His caregiving capacity led him to choose community organization as his major, and he started his work with immigrants immediately after graduation. He married a woman he met in social work school, five years older than he and once previously married with a five-year-old son. They had twins one year later, and their marriage lasted eleven years. As Karl looked back on it, he characterized the years as periods of shared delight in their children, heated fights about his feeling unappreciated, his certainty that his wife was only interested in him as a source of support for herself and the children. During periods of depressed resignation, Karl's job was his only source of gratification, and as social legislation began to erode funding for his agency, his depression deepened. His community organizational activities also escalated, and he used planning meetings as a place to vent his generalized anger, spending less and less time with his family. Finally, his wife filed for divorce, a step his own lingering religious constraints had prevented him from taking, and he did not contest.

Karl had been convinced that his third marriage would be a happy one. He had met his wife at a Vipassana meditation retreat. He had begun meditation practice after his divorce, because he hoped it would calm his agitation and his increasingly volatile temper. He liked the silence of meditation retreats and scheduled his vacations around them. His wife shared his enthusiasm for meditation, and they meditated daily together. She had seemed, when they met, more devoted and less needy than Karl's previous wives, but after two years of marriage, the old pattern of "non-reciprocated relationship" had emerged, with discussions quickly becoming battles, and Karl was distraught.

I saw Karl individually for several sessions and felt that he used his intellectual awareness of the source of his quick temper —"I keep falling for needy women, but they don't reciprocate my caretaking"—as a justification for fighting. He felt depressed to be in an ungratifying relationship and too immobilized to leave it. I then suggested seeing Karl and his wife together, in an attempt to see if they could both modify their behavior so that the relationship could continue.

I was impressed with Karl and Kathy as a couple. They seemed genuinely affectionate with each other, less adversarial than I had imagined from Karl's description. They eagerly accepted my suggestions for working with "Right Speech," a concept they knew from their Buddhist practice. They incorporated into their speech pattern my idea that anger arises when we are frightened, so that they would say, "When you seem uninterested in my needs, I am frightened that you don't love me."

Therapy sessions were spent reviewing fights that had occurred during the week. By reconstructing their feelings at the time, they were able to recognize the fear that had been the source of the anger. During our sessions, it was not unusual for either Karl or Kathy to burst into tears as they recalled a frightening time of their childhood. At such times, the other partner would respond compassionately, and all three of us would feel moved and hopeful that this level of mutual support would continue. Yet even when they left my office with strong intentions to never fight again, they would often report that the "truce" had held only briefly and that some seemingly minor event had precipitated a new crisis. Three months passed, and I felt we had not made much progress.

The adventitious event of Karl's suffering a coronary spasm, brought on by an episode of rage, was the turning point in the therapy. Although he did not need further coronary care, his internist insisted that he try Prozac for his depression and especially for his rage. I had suggested antidepressants at several points in the therapy, but Karl was adamantly opposed on several counts. His general mistrust of Western medicine was a strongly held value. He also felt that taking a medicine would make him the identified patient, and it would mean that he had failed in triumphing over his own mind, something he saw as a defeat. However, at his internist's insistence, he began Prozac (20 mg./day) and began to feel less depressed after one week. The most immediate result of taking the drug was the virtual disappearance of his quick temper. He continued to notice that he was upset, but his reaction was calm.

At this time, his therapy experience changed. His relationship with Kathy became smoother and more loving, and she decided to leave couples' therapy and continue her individual therapy with another therapist. I continued seeing Karl for one year, weekly, during which time he became aware of how profoundly lonesome he had felt during his childhood, how much he had missed, and resented, his absent father, and also how much he had resented his "special relationship" with his mother, which had left him feeling guilty and estranged from his siblings.

I feel that the Prozac potentiated the psychotherapy in two ways. As Karl became less wrathful, his relationship with Kathy became more loving and supportive. Also, the Prozac reduced his level of anxiety, so that unconscious material was emerging. Having previously been too frightening to experience, this soon became available for therapy. Another surprising result of the Prozac was that Karl's meditation practice thrived. He found that he was better able to maintain a focused attention and was less distracted by ruminative, depressive thoughts. His overall mood improved enormously, he felt more vigorous, and eventually therapy was terminated by mutual agreement.

Karl's taking Prozac clearly aided the therapeutic process. I find the judicious use of antidepressant drugs is an important adjunct to therapy when indicated. With many patients, however, there are "spiritual" antidepressants which I have discovered can be helpful. Practicing forgiveness, for example, can be utilized as an effective tool.

It may be easy to bring people to see the amount of personal pain they experience by holding on to a grudge, but it is not so easy to let go of grudges, even when one would like to. Again, all the major traditions seem to provide forgiveness practices. In the Buddhist tradition, practitioners cultivate *metta* (lovingkindness) through the recitation of wishes for the well-being of oneself and others. A simple version of *metta* meditation is:

"May I be happy, may I be peaceful;
May you be happy, may you be peaceful."

These resolves begin with wishes for oneself, for peace of mind and ease—the very repetition of the resolves acts as a calming agent in the mind. As the mind calms and the body relaxes, antipathy usually decreases, and natural forgiveness or understanding emerges. Even if one is too angry to say the *metta* resolve, "May you be happy, may you be peaceful," one can keep the focus on just oneself, i.e., "May I be happy, may I be peaceful." Repetition of that half of the resolve will eventually lead to a softening of one's anger toward the other person.

A central focus of Christian prayer is examination of one's own conscience and the wish to be absolved of one's mistakes, e.g.: "Forgive us our trespasses, as we forgive those who trespass against us" (Lord's Prayer, Matthew, 6:12). I have worked with patients using *A Course in Miracles* who found that they could let go of feelings of ill will by repeating to themselves the lesson, "I and my brothers are one with God."

Years ago, while on a retreat, I learned from Joseph Goldstein, the noted American Buddhist teacher, a forgiveness meditation which can be effectively practiced when anger arises in a relationship:

> *If I have offended or harmed anyone, knowingly or unknowingly, I ask their forgiveness—and—if anyone else [e.g., spouse] has offended or harmed me knowingly or unknowingly,* I FORGIVE THEM.

Initially, the words may almost be unutterable, but with repetition and practice, it does get easier. Any mind moment we spend being angry precludes our having a happy or loving mind moment. As with the metta meditation above, if it is impossible to verbalize forgiveness of the other person, one may keep the focus on oneself, and eventually the anger toward the other person will soften.

Recently, I came across a Hebrew forgiveness prayer that closely parallels that given to me by Joseph Goldstein. Recognizing that anger and resentment are antithetical to a peaceful mind, the last service of the Jewish liturgical day includes a prayer that begins:

> *Master of the Universe, I hereby forgive anyone who angered or antagonized me or who sinned against me—whether against my body, my property, my honor or against anything of mine—whether accidentally, willfully, or purposely; whether through speech, deed, thought or notion; whether in this trans-migration [incarnation] or another transmigration—I forgive everyone. May no man [or woman] be punished because of me. (Scherman, 319)*

If this is recited every night before bedtime, the tendency to carry grudges or harbor resentments will be diminished.

When I mention these practices to patients, I do so primarily in the spirit of inspiration. Some people actually begin to incorporate these practices into their lives. This usually happens when people are already pursuing a spiritual path and are feeling pleased to realize that they are doing spiritual work as they heal their relationship. Even when people do not actively begin a formal forgiveness practice, just hearing about the value of forgiveness is often inspiring enough to begin to make the direct expression of anger ego alien.

As more people begin to meditate and do things they perceive to be part of their spiritual life, problems may arise if the other partner has no positive interest in these matters. This lack of interest may stem from having had negative experiences relating to religion in one's childhood. What is actually more common is that the "spiritual" partner uses his or her "spirituality" in such a way that the other partner feels excluded, not valued, and even denigrated. It is important for the transpersonal therapist to see the most important issue here as being psychological problems that are using spiritual issues as a battleground. When lived properly, a spiritual approach to life should be loving and life-enhancing. (This same dilemma is played out on the world scene, where spirituality or religion is used as a justification for all types of destructiveness to others.)

Case Study: Theresa and Charles

Theresa and Charles had been married fifteen years and had two daughters. They consulted me prior to filing for divorce. Both had experienced severe early emotional deprivation at the hands of alcoholic parents. They handled their anxiety about having a committed relationship by carrying on many superficial extramarital affairs. Yet both also felt some type of deep caring for each other.

Charles was the spiritual seeker and Theresa was not. Charles earned his livelihood by giving weekend seminars on spirituality and teaching yoga. Theresa held a high position in a prestigious accounting firm. She was the practical one who micromanaged the family's finances, while Charles was the dreamer. Charles used his "spirituality" to berate and belittle Theresa about her materialism and greed (which in fact was an accurate characterization and her way of coping with a world of people she couldn't trust). Their fights were compounded by their mutual use of alcohol, resulting in rageful battles that exhausted them and left them feeling totally demoralized.

My knowledge of some of the aspects of Charles's spirituality, which was Christian-based, helped to break the deadlock. Traditional psychodynamic approaches could begin to be used when the "spirituality" was removed from the arena of the real conflicts. Being conversant in the great spiritual and religious traditions gave me the tools to focus (gently) on Charles's misuse of the spiritual approach in relation to his wife. Some traditional medicational approaches (antidepressants) helped make the forces behind their rages manageable and enabled them to focus and make progress with a traditional psychotherapeutic approach.

Because Charles saw himself as a "spiritual" person, I could urge him to honor some of the major tenets of all spiritual paths, namely Right Speech and Right Action, i.e., the use of skillful speech and action to help his wife feel cared for and understood.

Theresa's mother had wielded her stern Catholicism as a weapon to frighten and control her children, and therefore all spiritual traditions with their suggestions of how to improve relationships were rejected by Theresa without any consideration. As commonly happens when one of the partners refuses to hurt or punish in return (I could get Charles to practice Christian "forgiveness"), fighting subsided greatly and resolution of underlying conflicts could then begin. Traditional transferential issues were then focused on to reduce the marital tensions.

Both Charles and Theresa had been using each other to recreate a relationship with one of their parents. Charles's father, like Theresa, was an accountant and, again like Theresa, he had always tried to control Charles in a harsh way. Theresa's mother had denigrated and mocked her, a style/trait that was present in Charles.

Transpersonal therapists will need to be on guard, as they will often be sought out by patients or clients with "spiritual" issues. They must not overlook or ignore traditional issues, which may not appear as exciting to them.

As a final note, I want to mention the particular pleasure I have as a therapist when I help couples heal a relationship. Of course there is great satisfaction in helping individuals heal from psychological pain, but there is, for me, an *extra* satisfaction in helping couples reclaim a love they once had for each other that has become hidden behind fear and resentment. Part of the pain of a failing relationship is the partners' disappointment that the loving feelings they once had seem to be disappearing. My hope in working with couples is that restraint in the expression of anger will help their minds clear, so that their fears can be safely shared and love for each other rediscovered.

Chapter 10

Conclusions

THE VERY PROCESS OF ASSEMBLING these case histories, rethinking the dynamics of each situation, and explaining how I understand change to have occurred has clarified even further for me my motivation in writing this book. The most obvious motive is my professional conviction that people feel better sooner and therapy is facilitated by the addition of a transpersonal or spiritual dimension. Not at all secondary, and perhaps even equally obvious, is my personal belief that a spiritual aspect of human psychological functioning not only exists, but its discovery and accessing is integral to emotional growth. It was a combination of professional and personal convictions that inspired me to present these views.

In addressing therapists, my primary goal is to make the point, both for conventionally trained and transpersonally trained therapists, that neither approach need exclude the other. Both approaches, used simultaneously, enhance the value of the therapy. Even, and perhaps especially, if I have succeeded in making this point, I may be raising new issues for both groups. I am encouraging both groups to examine and possibly incorporate a point of view previously not important to them.

Traditional therapists are being asked to open their field of inquiry to include existential issues and spiritual concerns. Certainly, I am not the first therapist to do this. Ernest Becker eloquently presented this point of view in *The Denial of Death*. A less theoretical and more clinical approach was presented by Irvin Yalom in *Existential Psychotherapy*. Scott Peck, writing more for the lay reader than for the clinician, is straightforward in his inclusion of a spiritual dimension in *The Road Less Traveled*.

The problem for traditionally trained, nonspiritually oriented therapists is that one cannot *decide* to have a transpersonal point of view. An interest in philosophical issues must arise, at least in part, from within one's own experience. It cannot be legislated. Nor can one decide to believe in spiritual truths, especially if they contradict traditional scientific training, even if one is moved to do so. My goal, therefore, in presenting this material to traditional therapists is not to make converts, but only to suggest this area as worthy of their consideration.

On the other hand, I am challenging therapists whose training has been transpersonally oriented to consider the value of standard psychodynamic formulations as an additional tool for understanding psychological dysfunction. It really is a challenge, because many transpersonal belief systems present a context for understanding life's dramas on a larger-than-personal scale. For people whose understanding of cause and effect extends past one lifetime, the importance of an oedipal conflict, or deficient early parenting, or any other particular trauma might seem minimal. My response to these therapists is simply that my experience with using a psychodynamic formulation has worked for me, in providing both a framework for understanding what needs to be done for my patients and a technique to do it. Because I believe that we are multidetermined, I feel comfortable acknowledging possible transpersonal roots of current experience when a patient thinks or feels these are relevant. The most successful tool I have as a therapist, however, is being able to make interpretations or interventions based on the patient's life history. Using this tool, I can more readily explain a patient's experience and often liberate his or her psychological functioning. Conventional psychiatry and psychotherapy have been refined in recent years by discoveries in neurophysiology. The newest pharmacological discoveries, nevertheless, do not obviate the need to understand interpersonal dynamics. And I feel I cannot overemphasize the importance of the broadest possible understanding of emotional functioning, which would include biology and personal history as well as transpersonal factors. My personal commitment to the pursuit of spiritual growth, and my conviction about the central place this pursuit holds in my life, is what prompts me to address this book to an audience larger than only therapists. My hope is that it will be relevant and helpful to people in therapy, to people who see themselves as following a spiritual path, to meditators and interested non-meditators, and to spiritual teachers who often serve as psychological guides and counselors to their students.

In my experience, patients in therapy are often mystified by the process of therapy. Although a great deal of psychological sophistication may sometimes be a disadvantage (especially if it is used as an intellectual defense against the experience of an underlying difficult affect), some psychological mindedness is helpful. It enables the patient to be an ally with the therapist in working out the problem at hand. In other words, it makes patients aware of what might be important to talk about, how to recognize a resistance when it emerges, and how to work out the variety of feelings they experience toward the therapist.

I hope this book will inspire patients, who might otherwise be hesitant to do so, to raise spiritual issues in therapy. Sometimes this hesitation reflects a certain shyness, a tentativeness about admitting an interest in spiritual growth. In other cases, this inhibition may reflect a fear about spiritual feelings or interest. Western psychology supports religion in terms of church affiliation, but as yet it has not recognized spiritual dedication as part of "normal" experience. Perhaps this is a holdover from the "scientific" psychological formulation that posited that religious interest represented some regressive, infantile urge. I have endeavored, in this book, to make it clear that spiritual longings, while they may sometimes indicate unmet childhood needs, often derive from our most sophisticated level of psychological development. Transpersonal therapists welcome the inclusion of spiritual issues in the therapy.

I hope this book will be specifically helpful to people who find that their spiritual practice is compromised by the continued presence of troubling psychological issues. Perhaps one pitfall of spiritual belief and commitment is the assumption that one's spiritual practice will be a cure-all. In other words, one might develop the hope that faith, belief, and meditative zeal will enable one to resolve psychological conflict without working it through in a traditional way. Even if it is theoretically possible to eliminate ordinary emotional problems with extraordinary spiritual insights, it seems that a traditional psychotherapeutic approach is more direct. Indeed, psychological insights often seem more accessible than spiritual insights. My sense is that it is a much more efficient use of energy to use standard tools to resolve psychological conflict than to attempt to use a strictly spiritual approach to resolve emotional conflicts and traumas.

Spiritual teachers, because of the high esteem in which they are held, often find themselves cast in the role of psychological counselors. Similarly, psychotherapists find themselves addressing spiritual issues. This should not be surprising, since it is true that spiritual and psychological issues are inextricably intertwined. I feel, however, that important differences exist in the area of expertise between psychotherapists and spiritual teachers. Therefore, I believe it is important for all spiritual teachers in Western culture to be somewhat knowledgeable about psychological functioning. This would include the ability to recognize emotional issues that are beyond their area of expertise. It would be helpful if they were familiar with various psychotherapeutic disciplines to which their students might be referred when it seems appropriate.

Finally, I hope that I have included in my audience people who are neither in therapy nor involved in practicing a spiritual path, as well as those who might feel the need for help from a psychotherapist. These last several decades of the twentieth century have opened the consciousness of Western culture to the idea of personal change and growth. Words like "self-actualized" and terms such as "personally fulfilled" have become part of our standard vocabulary. Much more than the pioneer generations before us, we have been trained to be alert to our feelings, aware of our discontents, and more broadly educated to the idea that change in the direction of a more gratifying life is possible. I hope, therefore, that this book accomplishes the additional goal of demystifying therapy, so that people who might be aided by psychotherapy will be inspired to search for a therapist who can be helpful to them. At the same time, I trust that spiritual search and practice can be considered, not as an esoteric tangent to real life, but as a crucial ingredient of a fulfilled, mature life. My hope is that in working on personal change people will consider both paths, preferably simultaneously.

Bibliography

Becker, Ernest
1975   *The denial of death.* New York: Free Press.

Boorstein, Seymour
1996   Transpersonal techniques and psychotherapy.
                           Textbook of transpersonal psychiatry and psy-
                           chology. Scotton, Bruce W., M.D.; Allan B.
                           Chinen, M.D.; John Battista, M.D., eds. New
                           York: Basic Books.
1983   The use of bibliotherapy and mindfulness medi-
                           tation in a psychiatric setting. *Journal of*
                           Transpersonal Psychology 13 (2), 173–179.

Boorstein, Seymour, ed.
1996   *Transpersonal psychotherapy,* 2d ed. Albany,
                           SUNY Press.

Boorstein, Sylvia
1996   *Don't just do something, sit there.* San Francisco:
                           Harper San Francisco.
1996   Clinical aspects of meditation. *Textbook of*
                           transpersonal psychiatry and psychology.
                           Scotton, Bruce W., M.D.; Allan B. Chinen, M.D.;
                           and John R. Battista, M.D., eds. New York:
                           Basic Books.
1995   *It's easier than you think: The Buddhist way*
                           to happiness. San Francisco: Harper San
                           Francisco.

Erikson, Erik
1964   Eight Stages of Man. *Childhood and society.*
                            New York: Norton.

Gershon, Samuel
1996   Neutrality, resistance, and self-disclosure in an
                            intersubjective psychoanalysis. Paper delivered
                            to San Francisco Psychoanalytic Society,
                            February 12, 1996.

Gilberg, Arnold L.
1995   Self-disclosure: A two-level issue. *Psychiatric
                            Times.* December, 36–37

Goldstein, Joseph
1983   *The experience of insight.* Boulder: Shambhala.

Goleman, Daniel
1995   *Emotional intelligence.* New York: Bantam
                            Books.

Grof, Stanislav
1992   *The holotropic mind.* San Francisco: Harper.
1988   *The adventure of self-discovery.* Albany: SUNY
                            Press.
1985   *Beyond the brain.* Albany: SUNY Press.

Harding, Douglas E.
1990   *Head off stress: Beyond the bottom line.* London:
                            Viking Penguin.

Hendrix, Harville
1992   *Keeping the love you find.* New York: Pocket
                            Books.
1990   *Getting the love you want: A guide for couples.*
                            New York: Perennial Library.

Hixon, Lex
1989   *Coming home: The experience of enlightenment
                            in sacred traditions.* Los Angeles: J. P. Tarcher.

Khyentse, Dilgo
1992   *The heart treasure of the enlightened ones.*
                            Boston: Shambhala.

Kohut, Heinz
1984   *How does analysis cure? Contributions to the
                        psychology of the self.* Chicago: University of
                        Chicago Press.
1978   *The search for the self: Selected writings of Heinz
                        Kohut 1950–1978, Vols I and II.* New York:
                        International Universities Press.

Kramer, Peter D.
1993   *Listening to Prozac: A psychiatrist explores
                        mood-altering drugs and the new meaning of
                        self.* New York: Viking.

LeDoux, Joseph E.
1995   Emotion: Clues from the brain. *Annual Review
                        of Psychology* 46: 209–235.

Mahler, Margaret
1952   On childhood psychosis and schizophrenia.
                        Psychoanalytic study of the child, Vol VII New
                        York: International Universities Press.

Natterson, Joseph
1991   *Beyond Countertransference: The therapist's sub-
                        jectivity in the therapeutic process.* Northvale,
                        N.J.: Aronson.

Nhat Hanh, Thich
1992   *Touching peace: Practicing the art of mindful liv-
                        ing.* Berkeley: Parallax Press.

Osborne, Arthur
1990   *For those with little dust: Selected writings of
                        Arthur Osborne.* Encinitas, Cal.: Ramana
                        Publications.

Peck, M. Scott
1985   *The road less traveled: A new psychology of love,
                        traditional values and spiritual growth.* New
                        York: Walker.

Progoff, Ira
1975   *At a journal workshop.* New York: Dialogue
                        House Library.

Renik, O.
1995   The ideal of the anonymous analyst and the
                        problem of self-disclosure. *Psychoanalytic
                        Quarterly* 64: 466–495.
1993   Analytic interaction: Conceptualizing technique
                        in light of the analyst's irreducible subjectivity.
                        Psychoanalytic Quarterly 62: 553–571.

Rowe, Clayton, and David S. MacIssac
1993   *Empathetic attunement: The "technique" of psy-
                        choanalytical self-psychology.* Northvale:
                        Aronson.

Schachter-Shalomi, Zalman, and Ronald S. Miller
1995   *From age-ing to sage-ing: A profound new vision
                        of growing older.* New York: Warner Books.

Scherman, Rabbi Nosson, and Rabbi Meir Zlotowitz
1985   *The complete artscroll Siddur*, Sefard edition.
                        Brooklyn: Mesorah Publication.

Scotton, Bruce W., M.D.; Allen B. Chinen, M.D.;
and John R. Battista, M.D., eds.
1996   *Textbook of transpersonal psychiatry and psy-
                        chology.* New York: Basic Books.

Spitz, René
1946   Anaclitic depression. *The psychological study of
                        the child*, Vol 2. New York: International
                        Universities Press.

Spitz, René, and W. Godfrey Cobliner
1966   *First year of life.* New York: International
                        Universities Press.

Stolorow, Robert, Bernard Brandchaft, and George Atwood
1987   *Psychoanalytic treatment—an intersubjective
                        approach.* Hillsdale, N.J.: Analytic Press.

Washburn, Michael
1994   *Transpersonal psychology in psychoanalytic per-
                       spective*. Albany: SUNY Press.
1988   *The ego and the dynamic ground*. (Second edi-
                       tion). Albany: SUNY Press.

Wilber, Ken
1996   *A brief history of everything*. Boston and
                       London: Shambhala.
1995   *Sex, ecology, spirituality: The spirit of evolution*.
                       Boston: Shambhala.
1990   *Eye to Eye: The quest for the new paradigm*.
                       Boston and London: Shambhala.
1981   *No Boundary: Eastern and western approaches
                       to personal growth*. Boulder: Shambhala.

Wilber, Ken, Jack Engler, and Daniel P. Brown
1986   *Transformations of consciousness: Conventional
                       and contemplative perspectives on development*.
                       Boston: New Science Library.

Woodward, F. S.
1973   *Some sayings of the Buddha*. New York: Gordon
                       Press.

Yalom, Irvin D.
1980   *Existential psychotherapy*. New York: Basic
                       Books.

1975   *A course in miracles*. Tiburon, Cal.: Foundation
                       for Inner Peace.
1986   *The Dhammapada*. Translated by Eknath
                       Easwaran. Petaluma, Cal.: Nilgiri Press.

Index

Alexander, Franz, 16
Alter ego relationships, 16, 28, 114
Altered states, 3
Amygdala. *See* Brain, old
Anal character, 128
Anger
    and *A Course in Miracles*, 33, 58,
      59, 68, 69, 70, 102, 135
    and fear systems, 25, 37
    and *metta* (forgiveness)
      meditation, 6–7, 94, 95,
      167–169
    and spiritual traditions, 157
    and Vipassana meditation, 70
    appropriate expression of, 62
    attenuating, 63, 74
    awareness of, 76–78
    biochemical derivatives of, 37
    brain physiology and, 146–155,
      159–160, 162
    fear underlying, 145–155
    in psychotic illness, 52
    in transference relationship, 132
    medication for, 152, 166, 167
"Anger and the Fear of Death"
    (Boorstein), 37
Anonymity, 41, 42
Antidepressants. *See* Medication
At a Journal Workshop (Progoff), 20
Atwood, George, 18, 42

Balint, Michael, 43
Becker, Ernest, 2, 173
Behaviorism, x, xi, xiii
Beyond Countertransference
    (Natterson), 45
Bibliotherapy, 9
Bipolar illness. *See* Manic-depressive
    disorder
Blake, William, 54
Borderline psychotic, xiii, xiv, 31, 34, 89
    clinical studies of, 61–79
Boundaries, 52
    softening of, 30, 31
Brain
    new (neocortical), 37, 147–154, 159,
      162
    old (amygdala) (limbic system)
      (midbrain) (primitive) (reptilian)
      (survival), 31, 37, 146–154, 156,
      159, 160, 162
Brandchaft, Bernard, 18, 42
Brief History of Everything, A (Wilber),
    11, 31
Brown, Daniel, xiv
Buddha, the
    as symbol, 31
    idealization of, 17, 29
    teachings of, 29, 73
Buddhism, 19, 20, 27, 29, 109, 130, 163
    Theravadan, 30, 98

Tibetan, 19
Zen, 32
See also Meditation
Buddhist
concepts, 109, 130, 132
literature, 110
meditation, 121
philosophy, 121
practice, 20, 29, 30, 74, 166
teachings, 157
tradition, 29, 167

Christian
belief systems, 102
mystical tradition, 7
observance, 101
religious practice, 8
teaching, 7, 9–10, 168
terminology, 8, 28, 33, 64
Christianity, 16, 19
Cognitive Developmentalism, xi–xiii
Collective unconscious. *See* Jung
Coming Home (Hixon), 32
Common Boundary, 42
Compassion, xvi, 10, 166
as response, 146, 148, 153–155, 166
cultivating, 25
of spiritual teachers, 119
our basic nature, 109, 143
spiritual paths and, 18–21, 144
the Buddha as, 29
working on, 39
See also Course in Miracles, A
Concentration practices
producing calm, 4–5, 119
See also Meditation, concentration
Countertransference, 7, 41, 44–47
definition of, 44
Course in Miracles, A
and existential questions, 136
and Self Psychology, 27–30
as structure, 55, 57–60
attenuating judgmental thinking,
113–114, 168
daily meditations in, 64–66

developing compassion from, 19,
161, 162
emphases of, 7–9, 29, 35, 135
for severely emotionally disturbed,
33
for working with anger, 69–70, 100,
102–103, 157
similarities to Buddhist practice, 30

Death(s), 125, 136
fear of, 2, 96, 97, 138, 146, 151, 154,
161, 162
feelings of loss at, 121
preoccupying thoughts of, 112, 113
threat, 148
Denial of Death, The (Becker), 2, 173
Depersonalization, 137, 139, 140
Depression, 56, 66, 75, 77, 85, 86, 91,
112, 115, 119, 122, 128–132
and anger, 69–70, 71, 164–167
biologic etiology of, 81
existential issues and, 129–131, 138
pharmacological management of, xi,
81–82, 152, 166–167
See also Manic-depression
Depth insights, 6
Depth psychology, 5
Depth psychotherapy, 107, 122
Dhammapada, The, 157
Diagnostic categories, 6, 39
Dissociated, 39, 126, 139
Dissociative episodes, 76–78, 140
as defense against anger, 78
as spiritual experience, 39
Drug therapy, 56
See also Medications

Ego
alter, 53
attachments, 143, 155
auxiliary, 52, 57
boundaries, 28, 32, 33, 40, 52, 53,
56, 58, 60, 71, 89, 91, 92, 97, 106
building, 9, 79
death of, 37

defects, 56, 59, 61, 72, 77, 123, 126
defenses, 5, 119, 122
development, 9, 27, 32, 33, 51, 59,
    61, 68, 79, 89, 119, 154
disintegration, 62
    fragile, 59, 68
    functioning, 75, 81, 111, 120, 157
    ideal, xv, 97, 103, 133
    mature, 22
    observing, 66, 68, 72, 107, 117
    organization, 40, 54, 91, 106
    reintegration of, 65
    repression, 107
    strength, 17, 33, 61–63, 70, 79
    strong, 31, 52
    structures, 6, 52, 54–56, 66, 71, 74,
        77, 79, 90, 119, 123, 125, 126,
        129
    transcendence, 11, 60, 79
    well-consoldiated (well-functioning),
        35, 60, 107
"Eight Stages of Man, The" (Erickson),
    17
Eightfold path, 19
    Right action, 19, 170
    Right livelihood, 19
    Right speech, 19, 158, 166, 170
    See also Buddhism
Emotional Intelligence (Goleman), 150
Empathic (Empathy), xvi
    approach, 22
    in therapy, xvi, 18, 33, 34, 41–43,
        45–46, 70, 82, 92, 97, 105–110,
        113
    lack of response, 61–62, 67,
        109–110
    response, 150, 154
    Self Psychology view of, 16, 45,
        103, 105, 114
    with psychological pain, 45, 90, 92,
        97, 106
Energic drive theory. *See* Freud
Engler, Jack, xiv, 31
Enlightenment, 11, 17
Entitlement, 35, 89, 90

Erikson, Erik, 17, 52
Erotic fantasies, 117, 137
Existential Psychotherapy (Yalom), 2,
    174
Existential, xiv
    angst, 37, 125
    concerns, 3, 134, 138
    crisis, 131
    issues, xv, 9, 23, 27, 126, 129, 136
    problems, 111–112, 125–141
    questions, 113, 132
Experience of Insight, The (Goldstein),
    132

Fear, 140
    and depression, 122, 129
    and neurosis, 35
    as a child, 106
    as obstacle, 143
    basis of, 31
    behind anger, 37, 145–148, 151–155,
        157–162, 166, 171
    recorded in amygdala, 149
    response suppression, 149–150
    systems, 25
    treatment with *A Course in Miracles*,
        64
    See also Death, fear of
Fight or flight, 147, 149
    See also Brain, old
Fleishman, Otto, 43, 48
Forgiveness, 6–8
    bolstering self-esteem, 35
    emphasis on in therapy, 35, 79
    in overcoming anger, 78, 94, 135,
        168–169
    in spiritual practices, 19, 25, 58, 59,
        65, 69–70, 74–75, 90, 95, 102,
        113, 157, 168–169
    of self, 29, 65, 94
    practices, 82, 155, 160
    working on in family, 39
    See also Meditation metta; *Course
    in Miracles, A*
Free association, 36

Freud, Sigmund, xvi, 31
    energic drive theory, 15
    See also Psychoanalytic psychiatry
Freudian, 1, 2, 9, 15, 30, 81
    psychoanalysis, x

Gershon, Samuel, 46
Gestalt, 13
Gilberg, Arnold L., 42
Gilligan, xi
God consciousness, 8, 17
    See also Unity consciousness
Goldstein, Joseph, 132, 168
Goleman, Daniel, 150
Grandiose delusional thinking, 85, 86
Grandiosity, 81
Greenson, Ralph, 43
Grief, 39
Grof, Stanislav, 1, 2
Guilt, 25, 35, 65, 102, 164, 167

Harding, Douglas, 3
Hasidism, 3, 4
Hebb, Donald, xiii
Hendrix, Harville, 146
Hindu
    greeting, 53
    lineage, 86
    practice, 53
Hixon, Lex, 32
Home, D. D., 21
Humanistic psychology, 39
Huxley, Aldous, ix, 54
Hypnotherapy, 77

Idealized figures, 16, 22
Idealizing
    absence of, 67
    building psychological strength, 17,
        65, 72, 79, 95
    function, 29
    in relationships, 17, 62, 72, 99
    over-, 22, 33, 38, 76

Insights
    psychological, 1, 68, 176
    spiritual, 4–5, 19–20, 37, 38, 47, 75,
        93, 111, 176
Interrelatedness of all beings, 18, 19
Intersubjective field, 30, 47

Jesus, 17, 83, 85, 103, 157
Jones, Jim, 21
Journal of Transpersonal Psychology,
    ix
Judeo-Christian practice, 19
Jung, Carl, 1
    Collective unconscious, 2
Jungian, 13, 20

Keeping the Love You Find (Hendrix),
    146
Kohut, Heinz, xvi, 15, 30, 45, 105, 106
Kramer, Peter, 162

Le Shan, Lawrence, xvi
LeDoux, Joseph, 37, 150
Libidinal
    drives, 106, 117, 118
    issues, 76
Limbic system. *See* Brain, old
Listening to Prozac (Kramer), 162

MacIssac, David, 16
Mahler, Margaret, 52
Mania, 87
Manic
    -depressive disorder, 81–85
    episodes, 82–85
Mantra
    personal, 20
    See also Meditation, concentration
Mararshi, Rama, 3
Maslow, Abraham, ix
Medication, 57, 60, 84, 162
    anti-depressive, 34, 67, 152, 166,
        167, 170

anti-psychotic, 34, 83
Depakote, 82, 87
Haldol, 82, 86
Lithium, 82, 83, 85
Mellaril, 57, 82
Paxil, 152
phenothiazine, 51, 52, 57, 59, 62–65
Prozac, 62, 81, 152, 166, 167
Selective Serotonin Reuptake
  Inhibitors (SSRIs), 62, 152
tranquilizer, 51, 64, 67, 71, 77, 78
Zolof, 152
Meditation
and medication, 162
and repressed material, 35–36,
  121–123
Chenrezi, 19
concentration (mantra), 4, 33, 36, 53,
  54, 64–66, 68, 73, 78–79, 107
daily, 28, 29, 64, 135, 141, 165
for development of heart and mind, 3
group, 95
increasing ego strength, 17–18
metta (forgiveness) (lovingkindess),
  6, 7, 74, 94
mindfulness, 4, 30, 36, 37, 72–74,
  160
on awareness of suffering, 20
practice(s), xv, 4, 18, 19, 21, 35, 36,
  38, 41, 53–55, 68–69, 73–75, 93,
  95, 109, 110, 121, 122, 124, 126,
  130, 137, 140, 148, 150, 165, 167
retreats, 5, 29, 30, 33, 35, 36, 39, 67,
  68, 72, 73, 83, 93–96, 98, 99,
  107, 109, 110, 114–118,
  120–122, 129–131, 139, 140,
  163, 165
techniques, 24, 40, 78
Transcendental, 53, 55
use to avoid feelings, 38–39
Vipassana (insight), 4–6, 30, 36, 54,
  67, 68, 70, 73, 93–96, 98, 107,
  109–111, 113, 114, 116, 118,

119, 121–123, 129, 136, 138,
  139, 160, 163, 165
Zen, 123
Mellaril. *See* Medication
Memories, 54, 116, 117, 119, 121–123,
  129, 139
Menninger Clinic, The, 43
Metta, 74, 167
resolves, 168
See also Meditation, *metta*
Midlife
and path to spiritual transcendence, 157
crisis, 112, 136
issues, 113, 134
Mindfulness, 73, 98, 107
See also Meditation, mindfulness;
  Meditation, Vipassana
Mirroring, 16, 29, 53, 57, 62, 67, 72, 79,
  95, 99
function, 27
grandiose, 22
Mood disorders
clinical studies of, 81–87

Narcissism, 22, 31, 67, 85, 89, 144, 156,
  162
See also Entitlement
Natterson, Joseph, 42, 45
Neuro-physiological psychology, x, xi
Neurophysiology, 174
Neuroses, 15, 35
Neurotic issues (conflict), xiii, xiv, xvi,
  9, 31, 35–36, 125, 127, 135–136,
  137
clinical studies of, 105–124
defenses, 54
Neutrality, 24, 41, 46, 47
"Neutrality, Resistance and Self-
  Disclosure in an Intersubjective
  Psychoanalysis" (Gershon), 46
Nhat Hanh, Thich, 156
No Boundary (Wilber), 129, 134
No-ego, 9

Observing awareness, 73, 110, 119,
124, 130
See also Ego, observing
Oedipal
conflicts, 106, 109, 113, 127, 128,
174
fears, 106, 110
guilt, 108
issues, 76, 108, 118, 124, 129, 137
neurosis, 43, 123, 124
strivings, 110
wishes, 106, 108
Osborne, Arthur, 3
Overeating, 66, 101, 116

Paranoid
ideation, 65
system, 60, 63, 64, 71
Paranormal phenomena, 38, 112
Peck, Scott, 174
Phenothiazine. *See* Medication
Phobias, xi
Piaget, Jean, xiii
Post traumatic stress disorder (PTSD),
149
Post-neurotic, 9
Pre-neurotic, 35, 40, 66, 75, 125, 134
clinical studies of, 89–104
"Pre/Trans Fallacy, The," (Wilber), 40,
104
Progoff, Ira, 20
Prozac. *See* Medication
Psychiatric Times, 42
Psychic(s), 21, 66, 75, 76, 77
gifts, 68
phenomena, 66, 77, 79
powers, 3, 21, 66, 79, 161
Psychoanalysis, 10, 36, 119
Psychoanalytic psychiatry, x, xii, xiii,
10, 12, 15, 105
*Psychoanalytic Treatment—An
Intersubjective Approach,*
(Stolorow, et al), 18

Psychosexual development, 9, 38, 39,
60, 105, 125, 126, 127
Psychotic, xiii, xiv, xvi, 28, 31, 32, 33,
34, 38, 61, 82, 89
clinical studies of, 51–60

Rage
and pre-neurotic, 101
fear behind, 56, 160–162
in borderline patients, 61, 66, 69,
71–72, 74, 76–77, 79
reducing excessive, 51, 58–59, 74,
90, 148, 150, 152, 161
See also Anger
Repression, 5, 6, 35, 36, 107, 110, 119,
145
of anger, 78
of feelings, 6
of thoughts, 6
Right Action, 19, 170
Right Livelihood, 19
Right Speech, 19, 158, 166, 170
Road Less Traveled, The (Peck), 174
Rowe, Clayton, 16

Sangha, 29
Schachter-Shalomi, Rabbi Zalman, 3
Selective Serotonin Reuptake Inhibitors
(SSRIs). *See* Medication
Self Psychology, xvi, 12, 15, 16,
17, 18, 27, 28, 30, 45, 53,
57, 62, 65, 99, 103, 106,
109, 114
Self, xiv, 2, 9, 30, 155, 156
sense of, 17, 28, 38, 53, 55, 62, 72,
105
separate, 32, 60
Self-confidence
increasing, 30, 72
lack of, 111
Self-control, 69
Self-critical, 6, 94, 98, 108, 111, 113, 128
Self-esteem, 89

enhancing, 55, 59, 69–70, 100, 103, 110–111
job giving sense of, 57
poor (low), 8, 33, 35, 53, 62, 74, 90, 103, 106, 108, 116
Self-hatred, 8
Self-idealization, 47
Self-observation, 63
Self-respect, 21
Self-worth, 63, 65
Selfishness, 21, 185, 189
Serotonin, 152
Sexual
    dilemmas, 106
    drives, 105
    enthusiasms, 118
    expression, 45
    feelings, 105
    freedom, 164
    functioning, 131, 134
    impulses, 15
    objects, 101
    response, 118
    strivings, 105
Sin, 8, 28
Spitz, Rene, 52
Splitting the object, 61, 62, 76, 77
Stolorow, Robert, 18, 30, 31, 42
Suicide, 21, 48, 71, 76, 77
Superego, 6, 15, 97, 105, 130
Sutitch, Anthony, ix

Teaching stories, 9, 10
    Hasidic, 10
    parables of Jesus, 9
    Sufi, 10
    Zen, 32

Ten Commandments, The, 19
Ten Ox Herder Pictures, 32
Therapist burnout, 10, 21, 47
Touching Peace (Nhat Hanh), 156
Transference, 7, 25, 40, 41, 42, 44, 45, 46, 62, 69, 102, 118, 132, 155, 171
    assumptions, 42
    cures, 16
    distortions, 42, 48, 70, 154
    idealizing, 28
    neurosis, 43
    relationship, 24, 97
Transformations of Consciousness (Wilber, Engler, and Brown), xiv, 17
Transpersonal Psychology from a Psychoanalytic Perspective (Washburn), 11, 156
Transpersonal Psychotherapy (Boorstein, ed.), 10
Twinship relationships, 16, 28, 79, 114

Unity consciousness, 8, 32, 37, 53

Value system, 22, 99
Vinaya, The, 158

Washburn, Michael, 11, 156, 157
Wilber, Ken, 11, 17, 31, 40, 104, 113, 129, 134
Winnicott, Donald, 43

Yalom, Irvin, 2, 174

Zillmann, Mallick, and McCandless, 150